# Don't Forfeit Your Joy

by

Dr. Paul E Griffis

*Don't Forfeit Your Joy*

ISBN:

# Table of Contents

# About Dr. Paul E Griffis

Dr. Paul has a BA in Intercultural Studies, a Masters in Clinical Counseling, a PhD in Marriage and Family Counseling, accreditation by the NCCA (National Christian Counselors Association) and the AACC (American Association of Christian Counselors), and a certification in Equine Assisted Learning.

He and his wife, Velma, live in the Ozark Mountains of Missouri. They previously served as missionaries for 27 years in the Amazon rainforest of Brazil and Venezuela, working with the Yanomamö language group. Paul is a trained paramedic and an experienced linguist who speaks six languages. He also has 30 years of experience in teaching, counseling, and coaching both young people and adults.

Paul and Velma love the Lord and have a passion for helping people lead fulfilling lives that are pleasing to God. They are members of Branson Bible Church in Branson, Missouri, where Paul is the Minister of Music and an elder.

## Dedicated to:

*My wife, Velma, and to our children and grandchildren: Candy and Brady (Travis, Dylan, Ashleigh, Emma, Mbali, Max), Mike and Michelle (Jesse, Ian, Liam, Tahlia), Jim (Kyler, Selah, Maylin), JJ and Clara (Eliana, Carina, Sonia), and Jennifer and Brendan (Iris, Fox). Love all of you so very much and I am proud of each of you. Jennifer encouraged me to write this book.*

*I also want to thank Sarah Haas, an incredible, talented writer, for editing the book for me. She did an amazing job.*

# CHAPTER ONE

## *INTRODUCTION*

We are living in a time of incredible fear and anxiety, largely due to the coronavirus. It is the unknown factor that naturally encourages one to fear or be anxious. Fear of the unknown is real and a normal reaction, and this is an understandable time to feel it.

Nonetheless, we live in a world that is prone to anxiety and fear. The coronavirus is just one of many factors that result in anxiety, depression, and fearfulness—when it isn't the coronavirus, it's something else! We shouldn't beat ourselves up for feeling afraid sometimes, for fear is a God-given emotion. It is what we do with it that makes the difference. As 2 Timothy 1:7 says, "For God gave us a spirit not of fear but of power and love and self-control." That is true for us as believers.

Many people believe that their emotions and attitude about life are beyond their control. If a pandemic occurs, they have no choice but to live in chronic fear. What else can you do? When bad things happen, they remain trapped in negative feelings, from anxiety to depression and beyond. People who think this way have what is known as an "external locus of control," which means that they believe external forces and circumstances outside of them are what ultimately determine their own choices, actions, and well-being. They tend to get trapped in a victim complex.

Of course we're all going to experience every kind of emotion at different times, but the reality is that we are not slaves to either our emotions or our circumstances. 2 Timothy 1:7 doesn't stop being true just because the media reports a new reason the public now has to feel afraid!

The Bible encourages us to have an "internal locus of control," or a belief that no matter what happens to us in life, we *always* have the ability to choose what we will feel, think, say, and do. Obviously, we cannot control much of what happens to us, and our options about what actions we will take are often far more limited than we would like. But people with an internal locus of control realize this and still believe that the ultimate responsibility for their own choices and inner wellbeing lies with themselves, not anyone else, and can never be taken away from them. As Christians, not only do we recognize that we have the free will to make these decisions for ourselves, but we also have the Holy Spirit living inside of us and giving us the *power* to make biblical choices! Talk about having internal control!

Joy is one of the key battlefronts where Satan tempts believers to surrender our internal source of control over to our circumstances. In this short book, I will address what I believe to be God's viewpoint on this concept of not forfeiting one's joy, regardless of the circumstance. Circumstances don't define our character; how we react to them determines who we are. We've all heard someone say something like, "Don't let them take your joy," or, "Don't let Satan take your joy." The truth is that neither Satan nor anyone else can take your joy. Only you can forfeit, or give up, your joy.

No one can take our joy from us. Satan can't take our joy from us. He can only tempt us, which he does in many ways. As he presents us with a number of reasons why we should surrender our joy, he also tries to convince us that it's not our fault if we do so; our problems *robbed* us of our joy, and we're the victims here! We must remember that he is a liar and a deceiver. We—and only we—can forfeit our joy. John Piper wrote a great book entitled *Don't Waste Your Life*. I'd like to amplify that phrase and say don't waste your life by forfeiting your joy!

> Rejoice in the Lord always; again I will say, rejoice. (Philippians 4:4)

Many years ago, I heard an anonymous quote that says, "Some people bring joy WHEREVER they go, and others WHEN they go." I'd like to be one who brings joy *wherever* I go. We don't always like to take responsibility for our attitudes, believing that they simply "happen" to us and we can't help it. But when we see them starting to affect other people, that should motivate us to begin learning how to choose joy more often! We can either be a source of anxiety and anger for those around us or a source of peace, kindness, and joy.

It's important to make clear here that no one in their "flesh" can muster up joy or choose joy by pure willpower. This is where much of Christian discussion on joy falls flat, because if we merely tell one another to be joyful because the Bible says we're supposed to be joyful, then we're not helping people turn to the only One who is able to give us joy when we have none in and of ourselves. Relying on ourselves to muster up our own emotional strength will never produce true joy, only a fake appearance of happiness and denial of our emotions while inside, the storm still rages on. We can only make those choices because of God the Holy Spirit living within us, who gives us that power.

Therefore, if you have never recognized that you are in your fleshly nature separated from a holy God, we must begin there. Ephesians 2:1–3 says:

> And you were **dead** in the trespasses and sins [2] in which you once walked, following the course of this world, following the prince of the power of the air, the spirit that is now at work in the sons of disobedience— [3] among whom we all once lived in the passions of our flesh,

carrying out the desires of the body and the mind, and were by nature children of wrath, like the rest of mankind.

God is a loving God, and yes, God loves you. In fact, because He is also a just God, and because He can't tolerate sin in His presence, He made a way for you by sending God the Son—Jesus—to die on the cross for your sins and mine. Jesus had no sin. He lived a perfect life, and because of that, only He could truly satisfy the justice of the Father. He took your sin and mine upon Himself to satisfy God's justice. He is asking you to trust Him, to put your trust in what He did on the cross for you. Although we were among the walking dead, Ephesians 2:4–9 gives us incredible hope:

> **But God**, being rich in mercy, because of the great love with which he loved us, ⁵even when we were dead in our trespasses, made us alive together with Christ—by grace you have been saved— ⁶and raised us up with him and seated us with him in the heavenly places in Christ Jesus, ⁷so that in the coming ages he might

show the immeasurable riches of his grace
in kindness toward us in Christ Jesus. [8] For by
grace you have been saved through faith. And
this is not your own doing; it is the gift of
God, [9] not a result of works, so that no one may
boast.

Here are a few more verses that show the
combination of God's justice, mercy, grace, and love:

...as it is written:

"None is righteous, no, not one;
[11]   no one understands;
  no one seeks for God.
[12] All have turned aside; together they have
      become worthless;
  no one does good,
    not even one."
[13] "Their throat is an open grave;
  they use their tongues to deceive."
"The venom of asps is under their lips."
[14] "Their mouth is full of curses and bitterness."
[15] "Their feet are swift to shed blood;

<sup>16</sup> in their paths are ruin and misery,

<sup>17</sup> and the way of peace they have not known."

<sup>18</sup> "There is no fear of God before their eyes."
(Romans 3:10–18)

For all have sinned and fall short of the glory of God. (Romans 3:23)

But God shows his love for us in that while we were still sinners, Christ died for us. (Romans 5:8)

For the wages of sin is death, but the free gift of God is eternal life in Christ Jesus our Lord. (Romans 6:23)

For by grace you have been saved through faith. And this is not your own doing; it is the gift of God, <sup>9</sup> not a result of works, so that no one may boast. (Ephesians 2:8,9)

For God so loved the world, that he gave his only Son, that whoever believes in him should not perish but have eternal life. [17] For God did not send his Son into the world to condemn the world, but in order that the world might be saved through him. [18] Whoever believes in him is not condemned, but whoever does not believe is condemned already, because he has not believed in the name of the only Son of God. (John 3:16–18)

You and I were born sinners, disconnected and separated from God. We had no hope, as we were spiritually dead. We needed someone to bridge that gap. Jesus provided the means to bridge that gap by paying the penalty for our sin when He took our sin upon Himself, giving Himself up to die on the cross and rising again on the third day, defeating death. The moment we put our trust in Christ, the Holy Spirit comes to live within us, and He gives us the power to choose joy regardless of the situation.

We recognize that power, as we search the Scriptures faithfully and the Holy Spirit impowers us to live the Christian life, to please God. Our choices must not be made, based on our feelings. By faith, we must trust God and believe His promises. His joy is not elusive. He desires for our joy to be full.

Pop culture lies to us, and Satan lies to us, telling us that "happiness" is based on our circumstances. God says, "Despite your circumstances, you can trust Me and experience JOY!"

Jesus said in John 16:33, "I have said these things to you, that in me you may have peace. In the world you will have tribulation. But take heart; I have overcome the world." In other words, He's saying that, yes, you WILL have trouble in this life, but you can "take heart" because He "has overcome the world," and in Him there is peace. That's where my joy comes from. When we meditate on the goodness of our Heavenly Father, and reflect on the fact that, although we live in a broken world, Jesus has overcome the world in all that He did on the cross, and rising again from the grave to defeat death, the penalty of sin. My peace comes when I apply His Word to my life and take my burdens to Him and leave them there. (Philippians 4:4-8) We like to take our troubles to the Lord, but as we walk away, we take them back far too often. I can and must choose JOY!

Music moves me, so I often think in terms of songs and have a song for just about every circumstance. At my church, we sing a song by Sovereign Grace called "Sovereign Over Us" that says:

There is strength within the sorrow
There is beauty in our tears
You meet us in our mourning
With a love that casts out fear
You are working in our waiting, sanctifying us
When beyond our understanding
You're teaching us to trust
Your plans are still to prosper
You have not forgotten us
You're with us in the fire and the flood
Faithful forever, perfect in love
You are sovereign over us

You are wisdom unimagined
Who could understand Your ways
Reigning high above the heavens
Reaching down in endless grace
You're the lifter of the lowly

Compassionate and kind

You surround and You uphold me

Your promises are my delight


Even what the enemy means for evil

You turn it for our good

You turn it for Your good and for Your glory

Even in the valley You are faithful

You are working for our good

You are working for our good and for Your glory


This can give us perspective and help us choose joy!


In each chapter, I will address three stages that we typically go through on our way toward discovering joy in the midst of our circumstances:


The Struggle

The Change

The New Focus

# CHAPTER 2

## *FOUNDATION*

Many of us are familiar with Philippians 4:4, which says, "Rejoice in the Lord always; again I will say, rejoice." But it is important to understand the context, the life story of the Apostle Paul when he commanded us to choose JOY! Paul was in prison and had been for quite some time. The prisons back then were not in any way pleasant. Prisoners were often beaten and given meager food to eat. The environment was very unpleasant, to say the least. Yet in the midst of that horrible situation, Paul held onto his joy, and he commanded us to do the same.

Hebrews 12:2 advises us to look "to Jesus, the founder and perfecter of our faith, who for the JOY that was set before him endured the cross, despising the shame, and is seated at the right hand of the throne of God." Jesus is, without question, our supreme example to follow. He knew from the very beginning the coming events that were in store for Him. He knew that He was going to die a very painful, horrendous death on a cruel cross. His joy was in the end game. He knew that He was being obedient to the Father and would be seated in the place of honor at the right hand of God. He chose joy and focused on the big picture, fulfilling the will of the Father and looking beyond the present momentary circumstance.

Hebrews 12:3 says, "Consider him who endured from sinners such hostility against himself, so that you may not grow weary or fainthearted." As we focus our eyes on Jesus, we don't grow weary or lose heart.

James 1:2 says, "Count it all joy, my brothers, when you meet trials of various kinds." The Greek word choice here denotes that we are to be genuinely joyful. *Chara* denotes a sense of inner delight, inner gladness. It's not based on a feeling, rather a choice in spite of the circumstance.

Galatians 5:22–23 says, "But the fruit of the Spirit is love, JOY, peace, patience, kindness, goodness, faithfulness, [23] gentleness, self-control; against such things there is no law." The fruit of the Spirit is made of nine components, yet it is singular in nature. You can't just have part of the fruit of the Spirit; it comes as a package set! I find this to be a "thermometer" in my life that clearly shows whether I am walking in the flesh/my own strength or walking in the power of the Holy Spirit. I must choose one or the other.

As James 3:11 clearly states, "Does a spring pour forth from the same opening both fresh and salt water?" Have you ever smelled sulfur water? If a well has sulfur water, you can pump it for eternity, and it will never turn into sweet water. The reverse is also true. If a well is a good well with sweet water, you can pump it for eternity, and it will not turn into sulfur water. If I am not experiencing joy, then I am also deficient in "love, peace, patience, kindness, goodness, faithfulness, gentleness, and self-control." We must not forfeit our joy. Paul frequently encourages the churches to hold onto their joy, no matter what:

> And so, from the day we heard, we have not ceased to pray for you, asking that you may be filled with the knowledge of his will in all spiritual wisdom and understanding, [10] so as to walk in a manner worthy of the Lord, fully pleasing to him: bearing fruit in every good

work and increasing in the knowledge of God; [11] being strengthened with all power, according to his glorious might, for all endurance and patience with **joy**; [12] giving thanks to the Father, who has qualified you to share in the inheritance of the saints in light. (Colossians 1:9–12)

We want you to know, brothers, about the grace of God that has been given among the churches of Macedonia, [2] for in a severe test of affliction, their **abundance of joy** and their extreme poverty have overflowed in a wealth of generosity on their part. (2 Corinthians 8:1–2)

Finally, my brothers, rejoice in the Lord. To write the same things to you is no trouble to me and is safe for you. (Philippians 3:1)

Now I rejoice in my sufferings for your sake, and in my flesh I am filling up what is lacking in Christ's afflictions for the sake of his body, that is, the church. (Colossians 1:24)

## THE STRUGGLE

The specifics of our struggle to hold onto our joy often take different flavors as we find ourselves in different life circumstances. However, anytime we are having trouble choosing joy, some of the same core roots typically come up.

A constant theme regarding our struggle is pride, self-centeredness and self-focus. Our struggle is that we want to—or somehow think we can—handle all of life's challenges on our own. We think that God expects us to simply generate our own fruit by trying harder instead of recognizing that the only way to attain the fruit of the *Spirit* is to be controlled by the Spirit and rely on Him instead of ourselves.

Another common barrier to choosing joy is that we may at times buy into pop culture's concept of "happiness," which says that our joy is dependent on circumstances. As long as we believe that we are helpless, our emotions will control us instead of the other way around.

## THE CHANGE

To experience the liberating change of the Spirit-filled life, we need to surrender our hearts, our minds, and our will to the Lord and walk in humility as Jesus models for us in Philippians 2:1–11:

So if there is any encouragement in Christ, any comfort from love, any participation in the Spirit, any affection and sympathy, [2] complete my joy by being of the same mind, having the same love, being in full accord and of one mind. [3] Do nothing from selfish ambition or conceit, but in humility count others more significant than yourselves. [4] Let each of you look not only to his own interests, but also to the interests of others. [5] Have this mind among yourselves, which is yours in Christ Jesus, [6] who, though he was in the form of God, did not count equality with God a thing to be grasped, [7] but emptied himself, by taking the form of a servant, being born in the likeness of men. [8] And being found in human form, he humbled himself by becoming obedient to the point of death, even death on a cross. [9] Therefore God has highly exalted him and bestowed on him the name that is above every name, [10] so that at the name of Jesus every knee should bow, in heaven and on earth and under the earth, [11] and every tongue confess that Jesus Christ is Lord, to the glory of God the Father.

Only God can change the heart—but when we surrender to Him, He absolutely can! I have personally witnessed God change hearts countless times in working with young people and counseling married couples. They had given up, but upon realizing that there truly was hope in Jesus, they were able to experience joy once again.

We had a young lady come in whose father had walked out on the family, leaving them devastated. She was despondent, feeling abandoned. She believed that her father had abandoned her because she was unlovable. When she heard that there was a God who loved her dearly and desired to welcome her into a relationship with Him, she put her trust in Jesus as her Savior and became overwhelmed with joy. God changed her heart from sadness to joy. We have to understand that He is the source of our joy. We must reject the temptation to buy into our culture's deception and look to His Word for our guidance:

And you became imitators of us and of the Lord, for you received the word in much affliction, with the joy of the Holy Spirit. (1 Thessalonians 1:6)

Rejoice always, [17] pray without ceasing, [18] give thanks in all circumstances; for this is the will of God in Christ Jesus for you. (1 Thessalonians 5:16–18)

## The New Focus

To step into the new focus, we must get our eyes off of ourselves and "look to Jesus," as Hebrews 12:2 reminds us. Philippians 2:5–11 gives more details about what it means to fix our attention on Jesus. He emptied Himself in humility and chose the path of service, suffering, and even death in order to obey His

Father and offer us mercy, love, and forgiveness.
Ephesians 5:1–2 likewise reminds us, "Therefore be
imitators of God, as beloved children. [2] And walk in
love, as Christ loved us and gave himself up for us,
a fragrant offering and sacrifice to God." We discover
unexpected joy as we reflect on the humble sacrifice of
Jesus and join Him in laying down our own pride,
plans, and attempts to procure worldly happiness for
ourselves in favor of surrendering to God and the good
gifts that He has for us.

Now our focus changes with the right
perspective. It is true that if we genuinely focus on
Jesus, we will see everything else in its right
perspective. We trust Him in the midst of whatever
comes our way, knowing that He is sovereign and is a
good, good Father! Everything He does, He does to
bring pleasure to Himself. As Hebrews 13:5 declares,
He's not going to leave us nor forsake us because He is
all about bringing glory to Himself.

The Apostle Peter gives us hope as he reminds
us that turning our thoughts to Jesus leads to joy:

Though you have not seen him, you love
him. Though you do not now see him, you
believe in him and rejoice with joy that is
inexpressible and filled with glory. (1 Peter 1:8)

Remember that joy is an essential component of
the fruit of the Spirit, as Galatians 5:22–23 says:

But the fruit of the Spirit is love, JOY, peace,
patience, kindness, goodness,
faithfulness, [23] gentleness, self-control; against
such things there is no law."

This is good news, because it means that as we allow
the Spirit to transform us with His new life, we will
radiate with His fruit—and with His JOY!

# CHAPTER 3

## *JOY IN THE MIDST OF ANXIETY OR DEPRESSION*

A few years back, I was teaching on the book of Romans in our college and career class on a Wednesday night. I happened to be in Romans 5:1–5, which says:

> Therefore, since we have been justified by faith, we have peace with God through our Lord Jesus Christ. [2] Through him we have also obtained access by faith into this grace in which we stand, and we rejoice in hope of the glory of God. [3] Not only that, but we rejoice in our sufferings, knowing that suffering produces endurance, [4] and endurance produces character, and character produces hope, [5] and hope does not put us to shame, because God's love has been poured into our hearts through the Holy Spirit who has been given to us.

I was talking about how "suffering produces endurance (patience), and endurance produces character" and so on. I mentioned that, unfortunately, I couldn't think of a current example of this passage being played out in my life to give them.

That Friday, we received a notice from the IRS saying that we owed the government $24,000!!! Talk about panic and anxiety!!! I immediately felt weak and overwhelmed, and I think I projected those emotions onto my wife, Velma. We impact everyone around us, after all. The following week, as I was reviewing our previous lesson, I said, "I can now give you a current example of suffering," and I proceeded to tell them what had transpired with the IRS. I was still very anxious, and even as I was teaching, it suddenly dawned on me. I said to the class, "I need to practice what I preach," and I surrendered my anxiety about our financial situation to God. Immediately, I felt the peace that transcends all human reasoning that Paul refers to in Philippians 4:7. It didn't change the fact that we still had to deal with the IRS, but I rested in the Lord and chose to be joyful.

In the end, we still owed the government around $9,000, but we were able to experience joy despite the circumstance as we chose to trust that God would continue to provide for our needs as they came up, just as He always had. I was reminded that some things I am responsible to change, while many things are totally out of my control. I can leave the results with the Lord, not forfeiting my joy.

I mentioned in a previous chapter that Paul was imprisoned when he wrote his letter to the church at Philippi. It was out of that scenario that he wrote, "Do not be anxious about anything" (Philippians 4:6). He certainly seemed to have a lot to worry about: whether he would continue to have enough food to eat, whether he would be beaten or punished in other ways, when he would be released from prison, or if his imprisonment would eventually end in his own death (as we know that it did). But instead of trying to foresee the future or micromanage God's plan for him, he sat down and wrote the epistle that is commonly known as the primary book in the Bible about joy. Choose joy!

Paul was not the only one capable of leaning on God's joy in difficult times, either. He shows us an example of a church body that did not forfeit their joy despite hardship is 2 Corinthians 8:1–2, which says, "We want you to know, brothers, about the grace of God that has been given among the churches of Macedonia, 2 *for in a severe test of affliction*, their **abundance of joy** and their extreme poverty have overflowed in a wealth of generosity on their part." Notice that they were suffering from affliction, and even in their "extreme poverty" they gave from an "abundance of joy." Where is our focus? To whom do we look?

I have heard many times that there are approximately 365 verses in the Bible that tell us not to fear—one for every day of the year! Do you think God might have known all along that we have the propensity to fear, rather than walk by faith? Here are just a few verses concerning fear:

Fear not, for I am with you;
  be not dismayed, for I am your God;
I will strengthen you, I will help you,

I will uphold you with my righteous right
  hand. (Isaiah 41:10)

For I, the LORD your God,
  hold your right hand;
it is I who say to you, "Fear not,
  I am the one who helps you." (Isaiah 41:13)

Are not two sparrows sold for a penny? And not
one of them will fall to the ground apart from
your Father. 30 But even the hairs of your head
are all numbered. 31 Fear not, therefore; you are
of more value than many sparrows. (Matthew
10:29 –31)

When I am afraid,
  I put my trust in you. (Psalm 56:3)

Anxiety sets us up to forfeit our joy—or,
perhaps more accurately stated, anxiety is a *biproduct*
of forfeiting our joy. Peter tells us in 1 Peter 5:7 to
"[cast] all your anxieties on Him, because He cares for
you."

I coached varsity football and basketball in Panama City, Florida, whenever we were back in the States for what we called a "furlough year." After every five years that we lived in the Venezuelan Amazon, we would spend one year in the U.S. to recoup from the stress of jungle life. After one of our furlough years, Velma and I were back in Venezuela again. We had to come out of the jungle to Puerto Ayacucho, a frontier town on the Orinoco River, to do required paperwork. I don't remember why, but I was discouraged during that trip.

One night, I got a telephone call from one of the guys I had coached in football. The fact that he was even able to contact us was a miracle—only God could have orchestrated that! His message was, "Coach, I just wanted to tell you that I love you, and it's because of your ministry in my life that I am where I am today." God used that to encourage me and to choose joy once again.

When Velma and I were missionaries in the Amazon jungle of Brazil ministering to the Yanomamö language group, we had some Brazilian coworkers. One particular family had a somewhat "romantic" view of what their life among the Yanomamö would entail. They truly loved the Yanomamö and had a genuine heart for the ministry. Unfortunately, in a few months they became overwhelmed by the demanding people, resulting in a mental breakdown. They had not shared their struggle, so the rest of the team was not able to help and encourage them until it was too late. They began to have "tunnel vision" and could only see the present circumstances, forfeiting their joy.

The truth is that all of the team had a sense of being overwhelmed at different times. However, we knew that such was the nature of working deep in the Amazon jungle among tribal people, and we were usually able to rest in the Lord and choose to rejoice in what God was doing in the hearts of the people.

Anxiety can paralyze us, render us lethargic or irritable, or cause us to withdraw. But even in horrible situations, we can choose joy. It may not change the circumstance, but it's our perspective that makes the difference.

It's essential that we take anxiety and depression seriously. Young people in particular who feel a sense of hopelessness can check out on a whim and take their own lives, sometimes even without warning signs. There **is** hope, and we need to be aware of those around us so that we can come alongside and help them walk through whatever they are experiencing. I've mentioned before and will mention again that circumstances don't define our character; how we react to them determines who we are.

An emotional progression that often takes place begins with fear, which leads to chronic anxiety, which can then lead to depression. Despite the circumstance, we can choose joy! It is a choice.

I recently had a client come to me due to extreme anxiety, which led to depression. He had an executive job in a state college. After a change in the college presidency, the new president made some radical and abrupt changes, one of which was to replace the executive staff without rhyme or reason. It was devastating for my friend, and he began to suffer from anxiety and fear of rejection in finding another job.

In time, he was able to recognize his fear and anxiety and began to address it separately, as its own issue independent of his job search. Even though the circumstances didn't change, he refused to forfeit his joy. Many months later, it was actually discovered that he had developed a tumor on the brain, thus magnifying the anxiety. Thankfully, he is now recovering from surgery and will have a long recovery period. But the joy that he learned in the midst of his last trial looking for a job has enabled him to carry on with God's joy now, as he has faced the setback of a brain tumor and the surgery to remove it. He couldn't control the fact that he had a brain tumor and that it was affecting him strongly, but he could make his own choices to fight for joy instead of giving in or assuming that he was helpless now in facing his own emotions.

High-stress vocations can easily create an environment that leads to anxiety and depression. I know of several well-known, respected pastors and missionaries who have had to deal with anxiety and depression. Stress is a huge factor. Yet many of these same leaders are choosing joy in obedience to God's mandate. Their focus, "looking to Jesus," allows them to choose joy despite the stressful circumstances. Some have realized that it was necessary for them to take medication to normalize their chemical imbalance. They still choose joy.

Has it ever helped to forfeit your joy? Has worrying ever brought about positive results in your life? Did it ever change your circumstances? Of course not!

## THE STRUGGLE

Here, too, we struggle against pride, self-centeredness and self-focus. Again, we have the propensity to think we can handle it on our own. This can prevent us from reaching out for help or resources and keep us trapped inside ourselves.

We cling to our preconceived ideas, ignoring the reality of anxiety or depression, or declaring it as sin in every case, or we take the other posture of panicking and sometimes giving up altogether.

We may even erroneously think we are immune to anxiety or depression. We are all capable of anything and everything in our flesh. It is important to remember that God "opposes the proud but gives grace to the humble" (1 Peter 5:5). We often judge a person struggling with anxiety or depression as living in sin. That is often not the case. What we do with it determines whether or not it leads to sin. 2 Peter 1:3 says that God has given "us all we need for life and for godliness." We can choose to walk by faith, or we can try it on our own, which leads to sin.

Often anxiety and depression are caused by a chemical imbalance in the brain. If we don't address the physical and biological influences of anxiety and depression, then the chemicals continue to rage out of control and harm us despite our best efforts to address our emotions.

## THE CHANGE

Surrendering to God is absolutely essential to holding onto joy in seasons of anxiety because we can do our best to choose joy, but only God can truly change our hearts. To find our way back to joy, our thinking must undergo a paradigm shift, which will lead us into the new focus. The change takes place as we read and study God's Word so that we get to know Him and internalize the truth of His promises.

It also takes humility to admit both to ourselves and others that we are struggling beyond what we can handle on our own and we need help. But the change comes as we meditate on Philippians 2:1–11 and fix our eyes on the humility that Jesus Himself first modeled for us.

In the case of hormonal and chemical imbalance issues, there is a supplement made by Standard Processing called Cataplex G that works amazingly well for anxiety, PPD, PTS, or depression. I have seen it work effectively many times in even extreme cases. The advantage of using Cataplex G is that it has no side effects, has no residual effects, and is not addictive. There are many pharmaceuticals that work as well, but if you read the labels, often the side effects are scary. Most, if not all, are also addictive.

## THE NEW FOCUS

Our perspective affects our focus, which in turn affects our joy. Let's look at the metaphor the writer of Hebrews used when referring to Jesus and His joy:

> Therefore, since we are surrounded by so great a cloud of witnesses, let us also lay aside every weight, and sin which clings so closely, and let us run with endurance the race that is set before us, [2] **looking to Jesus**, the founder and perfecter of our faith, who for the joy that was set before him endured the cross, despising the shame, and is seated at the right hand of the throne of God. (Hebrews 12:1–2)

The metaphor here is that of running a race. It takes discipline to prepare for a race. One must train, resulting in agonizing pain. I ran track in high school and was incredibly competitive. I ran sprints, relays, and low hurdles and also pole vaulted. To prepare for a race, I would often "weigh heavy" in preparation. That meant practicing with heavier shoes, sweatpants, and sweatshirt. However, on the day of the meet, I would get as light as I could— "laying aside every weight" that would slow me down. Once in the blocks, my focus was completely glued straight ahead to the finish line. I felt light and free suddenly running without the weights, and vaulting across the finish line was a breeze!

Our new focus is now "looking to Jesus." We have to choose to focus on the source of all joy, and that is Jesus. If our new focus is on Him instead of the circumstances around us, we can choose joy. Even though Jesus knew the agonizing, horrible death He was going to suffer, He experienced joy because of His focus on the end game. The circumstances were not going to change, yet He chose joy.

Depression is real, and even though you may need medication to regulate your chemical imbalance, focusing on Jesus makes it possible for us to choose joy.

Choosing joy in the midst of anxiety and depression involves more than wishful or magical thinking, though; it also means doing the hard work of making healthy choices that help us open up to the joy that God has for us. Getting rigorous daily exercise is very effective in reducing stress, anxiety and depression. Listening to some good music also helps.

Turning off the news on the television and internet can decrease a lot of stress. The news media thrives by dwelling on negative news, because bad news sells. Not too long ago, the news used to be on once at 6:00 a.m. and again at 10:00 p.m. Now it's streaming 24/7, 365 days a year! It is no longer just a delivery of facts, either. Rather, it includes events, speculation, and arguing. It seems to exist just to get everyone worked up, and unfortunately, pop culture seems to not be able to get enough of it. We love drama and a good "train wreck." While keeping up with every high and low of the news seems desirable upfront, consuming a lot of news usually yields bad fruit of anger, fear, paranoia, cynicism, depression, and overwhelm in our loves—the opposite of the fruit that God's Spirit gives us!

Remember, joy is an essential component of the fruit of the Spirit. We must not forfeit our joy.

# CHAPTER 4

## *JOY IN THE MIDST OF LOSING A LOVED ONE*

It's overwhelmingly difficult to exercise joy after losing a loved one. However, even then we don't have to forfeit our joy. It's all about perspective.

I had an unusual childhood because my immediate family experienced a series of losses. My father died in a forest fire when I was three years old. My stepfather was then killed when I was a young teenager. I guess I thought that it was normal to suffer loss like this. Even at a young age, perhaps out of a childlike faith, I trusted that God knew what He was doing, and I chose joy. On many other occasions, though, I did forfeit my joy as I grew up and reflected back on the deaths of my father and stepfather, and I was miserable as a result.

When I was in the US Air Force stationed in Panama City, Florida, at Tyndall AFB, I received bad news: my sister, Judy, had died at the age of 25. She had a brain aneurysm and ended up dying in post op. That was devastating to me, and I found myself questioning God and His goodness in allowing that to happen. I most definitely forfeited my joy! As I prayed and searched God's Word for understanding, I came to the realization that God was sovereign, and He could see the big picture, which I could not. I was able to change my focus on surrendering my heart to Jesus, choosing joy in the midst of deep sorrow. The pain of Judy's death was with me for a long time, but at the same time I had genuine peace, knowing that God was in absolute control, and that I could trust Him, choosing to experience joy, while walking in the Spirit.

After serving my years in the US Air Force, my wife, Pam, and I volunteered to serve as missionaries in Venezuela, South America. We built a new life on the mission field; we moved there with our two kids, and our next two children were born in Venezuela. We gave everything we had to serve God in the jungle. After several years of hard work deep in the Amazon Rainforest, I woke up one Sunday morning to the realization that my wife had gone to be with the Lord in the night. I was brokenhearted, to say the least!

This was the most difficult thing I had ever endured. The hardship I had considered so commonplace as a child suddenly didn't strike me as being normal at all. I walked down the grass airstrip that cut across our front yard like a driveway (since the only way into the jungle was by small airplane, our version of the family car) praying, "Father God, I don't understand this. I don't know how I'm going to make it, but I know You are good, and I know You have a purpose. I trust You as my Dad." God gave me and the kids a "peace that transcends all human reasoning." I was able to choose joy, even in the midst of deep sorrow and grieving. I continued to feel a real sense of grief, but again, because I trusted God and His goodness, I found joy in resting in His promises. Even in the midst of deep sorrow, I was able to choose joy.

Losing a loved one is very difficult; in fact, it's beyond words. It's okay to miss that person and even to continue missing him or her over the course of time. The most difficult loss of all is probably the loss of a child. There's something written within us, a perception that our children should outlive us as parents. I had a very close missionary pilot friend who was killed in an airplane crash in the jungle. His wife was left with three small children. She grieved and suffered deeply, yet she experienced joy in the midst of it all. His mother said to me, "You understand what I'm going through," but I had to reply, "No, ma'am, I don't. By God's grace, I've never lost a child." She was in deep pain, but it was encouraging to witness her joy in the middle of it all.

One Yanomamö young man named Almir who was about fifteen years old suffered from cirrhosis of the liver. He was bitten by a bushmaster snake, and due to the preexisting liver damage, he was dying. Despite knowing that he was going to die, he was extremely joyful. In fact, he called all of his family together to tell them that he really thought God was going to take him home to heaven during the night. So he said, "If you ever want to see me again, you need to put your trust in Jesus." That night, at about 3:00 a.m., we heard him sit up in his hammock and say, "Father God, I'm ready to come home." Right after that, he lay back down and passed away. His joy was well known among the other young people, and it had an amazing impact on them. They experienced joy in the midst of their sorrow that Almir was gone.

Several years ago, I received a phone call in the middle of the night letting me know that my mom had gone to be with the Lord. My ringtone at that time was the chorus of the song "Here I Am to Worship" written by Tim Hughes and sung by Chris Tomlin: "Here I am to worship; here I am to bow down. Here I am to say that you're my God. You're altogether lovely, altogether worthy, altogether wonderful to me." How appropriate to put it in perspective that my mom was in the presence of God, no longer suffering. It brought me true joy to think of her being welcomed "home" by Jesus with a big hug. A great illustration of what that might look like is the painting *First Day in Heaven* by Kerolos Safwat, which shows Jesus squeezing a young woman so tightly that He's lifting her off the ground. Her face is stretched with deep, guttural emotion, and you can almost hear her screaming for joy as she finds herself in His embrace. Through this painting, Safwat helps us visualize the incredible joy and wellbeing that our loved ones are experiencing after they have left us to go home to Jesus—truly, they are not dead but radiantly alive!

Many women suffer deeply after they experience a miscarriage. It's often difficult for men to understand the pain and sorrow of a mother miscarrying. But it's absolutely devastating for women, which makes sense, since the unborn baby was literally a part of them but has now vanished overnight. Whether we understand what someone else is going through or not, part of helping those we love deal with their loss involves validating their pain (which is absolutely valid!), sitting with them, and listening compassionately as they express everything they feel. One form of loss may seem more crushing than another, but try telling that to the person going through it; death is agonizing every time it comes.

That's why it's so important to go through the grieving process. If we deny our emotions about death and loss, then we simply bury them under the surface, where they can gain strength until they're so big that they incapacitate us later on. However, even in the midst of that sorrow and grief we can also choose joy. In fact, we *must* choose joy! 1 Thessalonians 5:16–18 encourages us, "Rejoice always, [17] pray without ceasing, [18] give thanks in all circumstances; for this is the will of God in Christ Jesus for you."

There is never a circumstance in which we are exempt from choosing joy. Although the circumstance doesn't change, we can still be joyful because of Christ.

## THE STRUGGLE

It's natural to find ourselves struggling with forfeiting our joy amidst the deep sorrow of losing a loved one. As with any other pain or challenge in life, it's easy to look inward and try to cope with grief on our own. We also struggle to trust the Lord with the situation, since we may feel like He has betrayed us or taken away that which we needed; how do we know He won't hurt us again? Our tendency is to forfeit our joy.

## THE CHANGE

After the death of a loved one, grief can feel inescapable and permanent, and it's easy to think that our situation is now hopeless. But there is always hope for a new tomorrow in Christ. The only way to experience joy is to change our mindset. Only God can give us peace in a loss of a loved one. Our job is to turn to Him and ask for that strength and to focus our minds on what is true. We must stop forfeiting our joy.

In 2 Samuel 12:18–23, David experiences grief at the loss of his baby but then comes to a place of acceptance. "Now he is dead," David says. "Why should I fast? Can I bring him back again? I shall go to him, but he will not return to me" (2 Samuel 12:23). David found comfort by realizing that he would see his child again one day and focusing his energy on living in the present reality without him.

When a fellow Christian dies, we can hold onto the promise that we will go to him or her later, as 1 Thessalonians 4:13–14 says: "But we do not want you to be uninformed, brothers, about those who are asleep, that you may not grieve as others do who have no hope. 14 For since we believe that Jesus died and rose again, even so, through Jesus, God will bring with him those who have fallen asleep." A lifetime may feel like a long time to wait until we see the ones we love again, but as James 4:14 says, "What is your life? For you are a mist that appears for a little time and then vanishes." We will have eternity to spend with Jesus and our believing loved ones, and it will be here sooner than we know it.

What we have today that we will not have then, however, is the ability to make eternal differences in others' lives. Paul took this perspective in Philippians 1:21–26, where he wrote about his own struggle:

> For to me to live is Christ, and to die is gain. 22 If I am to live in the flesh, that means fruitful labor for me. Yet which I shall choose I cannot tell. 23 I am hard pressed between the two. My desire is to depart and be with Christ, for that is far better. 24 But to remain in the flesh is more necessary on your account. 25 Convinced of this, I know that I will remain and continue with you all, for your progress and joy in the faith, 26 so that in me you may have ample cause to glory in Christ Jesus, because of my coming to you again.

As we fix our eyes on Jesus and learn to love Him even more than we love anyone else, we find new reasons to carry on. Jesus humbles us by reminding us that He, too, was "a man of sorrows and acquainted with grief" (Isaiah 53:3), as He grieved after the deaths of both John the Baptist (Matthew 13:14,22–23) and Lazarus (John 11:33–35), but He still continued in His mission to love and reach others. This eternal perspective and faithful love for others yield a harvest of joy in our lives.

## THE NEW FOCUS

Once again, we choose to be joyful, knowing that our Heavenly Father loves us dearly and that He sees everything with perfect clarity. Our new focus is choosing to trust Him, even in this loss. In the midst of life's deepest sorrow, we choose to focus on the One who can give us peace. We choose to be joyful, remembering the deep sorrow He chose to take on, suffering a gruesome death in order to reconnect us to the Creator of the universe, who is now our good, good Father.

The New Testament never suggests that we are unable to produce the fruit of the Spirit in certain seasons, and joy is a critical component of the fruit of the Spirit. Though loss is undeniably painful, we rejoice in knowing that the Holy Spirit continues to indwell and empower us even in the valley of the shadow of death—and His rod and His staff are strong enough to comfort us even there.

# CHAPTER 5

## *JOY IN THE MIDST OF CHANGE*

Change is stressful, and major change is majorly stressful. Even big positive changes release a flood of stress hormones, as we must summon extra resources to brace for the unexpected and readjust to a new way of doing things. For some, change is a constant and reoccurring challenge, as many vocations such as the military, missions, pastoral care, and others must move, change jobs, or regularly make other major life changes. This can be disruptive to family life. However, we can choose joy in spite of the stress of making major changes in our lives.

Moving to Venezuela as missionaries was easy for my wife and me, in the sense that we were committed to ministry. However, that was not the case with some of her family. They most definitely forfeited their joy because of the change in location when their daughter chose to move overseas with their two grandchildren. With time, I think they were able to work through it and find peace in God's grace. They chose joy even though the circumstances didn't change.

When Velma and I married, we made the change from Venezuela to Brazil, though we continued working with people in the Yanomamö language group. Though the language stayed the same, many other key aspects of our lives underwent an abrupt shift. It was difficult for our kids to change schools. It was difficult for us to leave Venezuela. At times, our family forfeited our joy, but more often we chose joy during the move. Velma and I trusted that it was God's orchestration for us to work with the Yanomamö in Brazil, so we chose to be joyful. It was probably more difficult for the kids, however they are extremely resilient, had great attitudes, and God gave them many opportunities to minister in Puraquequara.

Upon completing almost 30 years of overseas ministry, we decided it was time to make a change yet again. It was a difficult decision, especially because I had no idea what we were going to do next. I still wanted to be in ministry. I would like to tell you that I always chose joy, but unfortunately, there were moments of forfeiting my joy in worrying about our future as a family.

We had always had a heart for ministering to families and to struggling teens. Upon returning to the United States, we founded and operated New Hope Wilderness Camp, using horses to work with these families. There were many difficult times, yet we witnessed God's constant provision and faithfulness. He did some amazing things in these young people's lives.

After 16 years of running the program, we felt led to change our ministry emphasis yet again. For me, stopping the program was an extremely difficult decision. Still, we were able to choose joy by recognizing God's will, God's grace. We had seen God work in the camp and touch many people's lives for 16 years, but we recognized that if He were moving in new directions now, then our job was simply to obey and trust that He had something new up His sleeve.

We then began an online counseling ministry called New Hope Counseling, which you can find at drpaulgriffis.com. Since closing the camp, we have been trying to sell our house and ranch for just over two years now. It has been tempting several times to forfeit our joy. We found ourselves discouraged sometimes—resulting in forfeiting our joy. We have to remind ourselves and one another often that God is in control and that we will sell the ranch in His timing. We speak Scripture to our own hearts, saying, "Rejoice in the Lord always; again I will say, rejoice" (Phil. 4:4).

We are presently under quarantine from Covid-19. I am a people-oriented person, so this is very difficult for me. But this, too, shall soon pass. I have to intentionally choose joy. It's far too easy to focus on the present circumstance instead of choosing to be joyful despite the situation.

Whatever change you are presently going through, know that you can choose joy. Choosing to forfeit your joy, worrying, or stressing out will **never** yield positive results for your life. The fruit of the Spirit, on the other hand, results in a harvest of righteousness. We can weather seasons of stress and change by choosing to hold onto joy even as we face the unknown.

## THE STRUGGLE

Most of us like the thought of security. We don't like the idea of change, the uncertainty of the future, or the unknown. During times of stability, it is easier to believe that we are in charge of what happens to us and to put our trust in our life circumstances. Change forces us to face how frightening and unpredictable life really is and how little control we often have over it. We struggle to rest in nothing more than God's grace and His goodness.

## THE CHANGE

We must humble ourselves and get our eyes off ourselves and onto God's plan for our lives. It's easy to put all of our joy and satisfaction in getting what we want, and our culture reinforces this tendency by telling us that we should expect life to hand us each and every one of our dreams. However, the Bible never defines the good life as one in which we get each of our desires met.

Instead, God wants each one of us to lead lives principally defined by justice and mercy, as Micah 6:8 states: "He has told you, O man, what is good;

and what does the Lord require of you but to do justice, and to love kindness, and to walk humbly with your God?" The main goal of our lives is simply for us to know and love Christ better and be transformed by Him. Paul explains this in Colossians 2:2–4, where he tells the church at Colossae, "Set your minds on things that are above, not on things that are on earth. ³ For you have died, and your life is hidden with Christ in God. ⁴ When Christ who is your life appears, then you also will appear with him in glory." Our lives certainly include work, education, family, health, and a place to live, but our lives do not consist of anything here on this earth because we have already died to this world. Christ Himself is now our life, and we must therefore set our minds on Him.

As we do so, we find the freedom to surrender to the plan that God has for us, trusting that it is good even if it doesn't feel good all the time. I don't think Joseph was very excited about God's plan for his life when his brothers sold him into slavery, but multiple nations rejoiced when God used his presence in Egypt to bring about deliverance from severe famine. Joseph was now able to recognize God's hand in his painful journey and tell his brothers, "As for you, you meant evil against me, but God meant it for good, to bring it about that many people should be kept alive, as they are today" (Genesis 50:20). We don't know what God is working in the events of our lives, but we can always trust that He is continuing to use it all for good (Romans 8:28).

## THE NEW FOCUS

Our new focus is choosing joy, knowing that God is good and He is always with us. Even as we learn that we cannot rely on our life circumstances to remain the same or to uphold us, we are able to lean in ever closer to relying on God Himself as our source of stability and security. Like Abraham wandering through Canaan with no clear destination or the Israelites in the desert never knowing how many days the cloud of smoke and pillar of fire would rest in that location before God chose to lead them onward again (Exodus 40:34–38), we can welcome change as a necessary teacher that equips us to know God deeper as we turn to *Him* to lead us through life instead of relying on our own plans or expectations.

Hebrews 11:13 speaks about those biblical heroes who "acknowledged that they were strangers and exiles on the earth." It can be easy for us to read that verse quickly and simply tip our hats at their faraway, ancient glow, impressed by their valiance but assuming that it doesn't have anything to say to us. After all, the majority of us will never leave our homelands and live in other countries for the sake of our faith, as Hebrews 11 speaks about both Abraham and Moses choosing to do. But change of all kinds invites us to adopt the same spiritual posture as the heroes of the faith as we, too, learn to place our hope not in the dream life that we wish to build for ourselves on the earth but in God's kingdom yet to come, as Hebrews 11 continues:

> For people who speak thus make it clear that they are seeking a homeland. [15] If they had been thinking of that land from which they had gone out, they would have had opportunity to return. [16] But as it is, they desire a better

country, that is, a heavenly one. Therefore God is not ashamed to be called their God, for he has prepared for them a city. (Hebrews 11:14–16)

Whether or not the changes that we face are geographical, they can all tempt us to want to crawl back into the past situation we are leaving—even if the past was broken, it was still familiar and therefore less frightening. A godly perspective on change, however, orients us away from focusing on controlling our outer situation and toward our hope in the heavenly city that God has prepared for us and on our relationship with God Himself. *He* is our destination, our anchor, our faithful shield, our goal, and our reward! As we choose to pull our hearts away from their obsession on the here and now and redirect them toward Jesus, we are set free from slavery to our circumstances and enabled to live in unchanging joy.

One of the ways in which change invites us to adapt our focus in life is to align our life goals with God's instead of leaving them trapped in the cage of our own desire for satisfaction. We learn that we cannot control what shape our lives take from season to season, but we can be instruments of God's truth and mercy to those around us no matter what happens to us. Little by little, we begin to long for the redemption of all people more than we long for our own wish fulfillment. We have a new perspective as we begin to feel God's desire to take the gospel to the ends of the earth. What an honor—we get to be a part of His overall plan! We get to represent Jesus. As 2 Corinthians 5:11–21 says:

> Therefore, knowing the fear of the Lord, we persuade others. But what we are is known to God, and I hope it is known also to your conscience. [12] We are not commending ourselves to you again but giving you cause to boast about us, so that you may be able to answer those who boast about outward appearance and not about what is in the heart. [13] For if we are beside ourselves, it is for God; if we are in our right mind, it is for you. [14] For the love of Christ controls us, because we have concluded this: that one has died for all, therefore all have died; [15] and he died for all, that those who live

might no longer live for themselves but for him who for their sake died and was raised.

16 From now on, therefore, we regard no one according to the flesh. Even though we once regarded Christ according to the flesh, we regard him thus no longer.17 Therefore, if anyone is in Christ, he is a new creation. The old has passed away; behold, the new has come. 18 All this is from God, who through Christ reconciled us to himself and **gave us** the ministry of reconciliation; 19 that is, in Christ God was reconciling the world to himself, not counting their trespasses against them, and **entrusting to us** the message of reconciliation. 20 Therefore, we are ambassadors for Christ, God making his appeal through us. We implore you on behalf of Christ, be reconciled to God. 21 For our sake he made him to be sin who knew no sin, so that in him we might become the righteousness of God.

At first, it may sound like drudgery or mandated labor to participate in God's harvest fields instead of chasing the dreams that we ourselves had. But Jesus said that "whoever would save his life will lose it, but whoever loses his life for my sake will find it" (Matthew 16:25). As we give ourselves, our dreams, and our sense of stability as a wholehearted offering to God, we are surprised by the joy He gives us back, often in the very activities we had once feared would be the death of us. Love becomes joy; speaking courageously about Jesus brings joy; serving in the most humiliating ways—without any recognition or thanks—brings the joy of knowing that we were a blessing to someone else and that we are walking in step with our Maker.

When Paul writes about his joy, it is often in connection with the churches themselves, as he says in Philippians 1:3–7:

> I thank my God in all my remembrance of you, [4] always in every prayer of mine for you all making my prayer **with joy**, [5] because of your partnership in the gospel from the first day

until now. [6] And I am sure of this, that he who began a good work in you will bring it to completion at the day of Jesus Christ. [7] It is right for me to feel this way about you all, because I hold you in my heart, for you are all partakers with me of grace, both in my imprisonment and in the defense and confirmation of the gospel.

Watching the church grow in spiritual maturity brought joy. Holding them in his heart with loving care was a joy. Paul endured constant travel and change in order to minister throughout the Roman Empire, but like Jesus, he pressed on "for the joy that was set before him" (Hebrews 12:2), fixing his eyes not on present stability and the worldly appearance of security but on the consistency of the love of God and the far more enduring satisfaction of seeing others be transformed through the grace of Jesus.

# CHAPTER 6

## *JOY IN THE MIDST OF FAMILY LIFE*

It's all well and good to talk about the abstract idea of joy, but those of us who live with families know that it's something else entirely to consider maintaining steady, patient joy day in and day out among our spouse and kids! What is it about the ones we love the most that can make the concept of unbreakable joy sound like an impossible ideal, a sappy version of Sunday school theology out of touch with reality? But no matter what the specifics of our home lives, we are *not* destined to snap at one another in a hopeless cycle. Joy is possible among our families, too! Jesus always makes a way for us to choose joy.

I am not going to delve too deeply in this chapter into the specifics of everything it means to have a healthy relationship with your spouse and children. If you would like to read a more in-depth biblical perspective on marriage and many issues that relate to the family, I encourage you to read my book *Modeling Family God's Way*, which you can find on

Amazon. For now, I will highlight a few key points on family dynamics and what it looks like to embody real joy in the home.

## Spouse

These days, the concept of what marriage even means is rapidly disintegrating, and even for those who know that marriage is to be between a man and a woman are still prone to absorbing the culture's subtler lies about marriage—like it exists for our own happiness or satisfaction, or it should always exist in a fantasized dream state without requiring any work or sacrifice, or the man and woman do not have specific responsibilities to each other. These false concepts of marriage sound on the surface level like they will lead to the path of increased freedom and happiness, but don't be fooled! Any way that opposes God's way is like the adulteress in Proverbs 5:3–6:

> For the lips of a forbidden woman drip honey,
>     and her speech is smoother than oil,
> ⁴ but in the end she is bitter as wormwood,

sharp as a two-edged sword.

⁵ Her feet go down to death;

her steps follow the path to Sheol;

⁶ she does not ponder the path of life;

her ways wander, and she does not know it.

Upfront, the philosophy of our culture and its pursuit of happiness looks appealing, but it only leads to broken marriages filled with grief. To find joy within marriage, we must pay close attention to what God says about how it should look.

God has designed marriage according to certain principles, and He has not changed that design. It speaks to His very character. It's reassuring to note that He is "the same today, yesterday and forever" (Hebrews 13:8). He is immutable! His design of marriage is very special, but maintaining our joy in marriage is a challenge.

As single people, we have more control over choosing our own independence and doing absolutely everything "my way," as Frank Sinatra sang. But when we enter into marriage, we are suddenly forced to compromise and sacrifice many of our own preferences because of all the differences between us. We are still unique in our individuality, but we "become one flesh" (Genesis 2:24). Someone told me years ago, "No two people think exactly alike, unless one is doing all the thinking for the other." This is certainly true. At the same time, it is interesting that the longer we are married, the more alike we actually think as we slowly build more and more shared values and lifestyle habits. Even so, we never become identical, and we will never stop having to learn more about each other and find new ways to flexibly adjust for the benefit of our spouse. No wonder it's too easy in difficult times to forfeit our joy!

God commands husbands to "love your wife, as Christ loves the church" (Ephesians 5:25). We as husbands have the responsibility to model "love, JOY, peace..." and the rest of the fruit of the Spirit for our wives. God has given us as husbands the responsibility to lead our homes according to His principles. When we choose to be joyful, it impacts the rest of the family in a positive way.

Both husband and wife need to walk through marriage humbly, serving and respecting each other.

It is imperative that we communicate well with each other as spouses. That means that we intentionally listen carefully to try to understand each other's perspective.

Ephesians 5:21 says that the model for any Christian relationship, including marriage, is "submitting to one another out of reverence for Christ." As couples, we need to choose to be unselfish in our thinking and prefer each other in love. If we choose to be joyful, we will encourage each other to choose joy. Joy is infectious.

When I first got married, I was very selfish and inconsiderate, although I didn't realize it at the time. If someone had asked me, I would have told them that I was a pretty good husband. I would work hard all day and then go play sports with friends, knowing that when I asked my wife if she was okay with it, she would say it was not a problem. She, on the other hand, was unselfish and very considerate, and I, being immature, took advantage of her kindness. I never realized that then, but in looking back, it's pretty clear.

The Lord had a way of bringing me back to reality when our oldest daughter, Candy, was born ten months into our marriage. That definitely helped me grow up! Candy was, and is, such an incredible joy!! Obviously, though, a newborn presented new difficulties that forced me to take on more responsibility. I encourage new married couples in pre-marriage counseling and marriage counseling to wait two years before having children to allow them to get to know each other better as a good rule of thumb. Even though Pam and I didn't have that time, Candy's birth helped me become more considerate and selfless. My wife's choice to be joyful from the beginning of our marriage most certainly impacted me.

Marriage is a partnership, and we are to model Jesus for our children through the way we honor and give preference to each other. When we choose to be joyful, we model joy for each other and for our children.

It takes considerable work to maintain a happy relationship. Choosing joy in the midst of struggles encourages a healthy home environment.

# Children

Our kids are most likely to follow what they see in us as parents. If we don't forfeit our joy, they will tend to be happier as well. It always amazes me that we require our kids to have good attitudes, speak kindly, and respond lovingly when often we don't model that well in their presence. Would you say that is a double standard?

Here is an interesting trend: in homes where both parents are present in the mornings when the kids get up and when the kids go to bed at night, a very small number of kids become juvenile delinquents. Our children tend to be happier when they are in a joyful, more connected atmosphere at home. Often, troubled and unhappy kids are in need of an adjustment in parenting.

However, that is not always the case, so we have to be careful not to judge others. We have some close friends who are faithful, godly parents yet have one teenager who is extremely rebellious. They've done everything possible to get him help, but he has rejected help. They get a lot of **unjust** criticism, and of course that is very discouraging and disheartening. My advice to them is to tune out unjust criticism and choose joy. Every individual ultimately makes his or her own decisions. The book *When Good Kids Make Bad Choices* by Elyse Fitzpatrick and Jim Newheiser is encouraging for hurting parents dealing with that situation.

In many cases, however, finding resolution and healing for troubled kids involves better choices that both the young people themselves and their parents can make. We have had close to 1,000 young people come through our counseling program. All of them came with a bad perspective of life and were very unhappy. The vast majority left here with a joyful attitude. In most cases, we were able to work not only with the teens at camp but also with the family to make necessary adjustments at home.

That investment may sound like a lot of work, but it yields a harvest of increased joy for children and parents alike. Proverbs 10:1 tells us, "A wise son brings joy to his father, but a foolish son brings grief to his mother" (New International Version). The Apostle John echoes this sentiment in 3 John 1:4, where he says, "I have no greater joy than to hear that my children are walking in the truth." John is talking here about his spiritual children, but it is equally true for us as physical parents when our children are walking with Jesus—pure joy! This doesn't just happen on it own. It's our responsibility as parents to teach and model a lifestyle of walking with Jesus. Please don't forfeit your joy!

Tragically, the suicide rate among young people is extremely high. Adolescents are going through huge hormonal changes, and peers can be extremely mean. Unfortunately, they are often emotionally fragile and can develop a sense of hopelessness, resulting in them taking their own lives way too often. It's imperative that we as parents invest in our children's lives by spending time with them. We can't get to know them and their struggles without being there for them. Most young people who live in a safe, happy environment at home feel secure and joyful. Again, it's important to note that every individual ultimately makes his or her own choices, so parents should not blame themselves for decisions that their children make. Rather, we should strive to do everything in our power to provide for them emotionally as well as physically and influence them towards life and wholeness.

Deuteronomy 6:5–7 sheds more light on what it means to raise children in an environment centered around knowing and loving the Lord:

> You shall love the LORD your God with all your heart and with all your soul and with all your might. [6] And these words that I command you today shall be on your heart. [7] You shall teach them diligently to your children, and shall talk of them when you sit in your house, and when you walk by the way, and when you lie down, and when you rise.

We are teaching our children by our very lifestyle. What we truly believe is what we do. Our actions are a direct reflection of what's in our hearts.

## THE STRUGGLE

We struggle with modeling joy well to our spouses and children. They may push our buttons and cause us to snap, or we may withdraw from family time to hide in isolation, or we may be out of energy and zapped by life's frustrations every day when we come home. The inability to work through conflict well, express our needs, or forgive can put a strain on our marriage or relationship with our kids, and many families get caught in cycles of fights or passive-aggression.

We may talk to our kids about the joy of the Lord, but we struggle with being hypocritical and living out an ethic of "do as I say, not as I do."

## THE CHANGE

It can be challenging to hold onto and demonstrate joy at home, where everyone can see into the inner crevices of our lives and we tend to live with our guard down. But this simply gives us the opportunity to make our joy *genuine* as it springs up from the inside out, regardless of whether we're dressed up and out in public or in our pajamas in the living room. True joy will continue in every place, circumstance, and relationship.

The best way we can serve our spouse and children and lead them into real joy is by cultivating our own intimate relationship with Christ. Jesus says in Matthew 10:37, "Whoever loves father or mother more than me is not worthy of me, and whoever loves son or daughter more than me is not worthy of me." Of course this doesn't mean that we shouldn't love our family members; we should simply love Jesus that much *more*! David gives us words for this in Psalm 42:1–2:

> As a deer pants for flowing streams,
>      so pants my soul for you, O God.
> ² My soul thirsts for God,
>      for the living God.
> When shall I come and appear before God?

As we press in to spending more and more time with Jesus, we are transformed by His joy, and our families will notice.

It is also important that we keep God's perspective on our families in order to maintain our joy among them. As Philippians 2:1–11 explains, we must remain humble as we imitate Jesus in preferring the interests of our family members above our own. Family certainly isn't always easy or comfortable. But as we shift our focus to serving them and pointing them toward Jesus instead of expecting them to serve as sources of happiness and wish fulfillment for us, we learn to find joy not in leading a family life without bruises but in caring for them and fighting for their good.

## THE NEW FOCUS

Our new focus is to model Jesus well by demonstrating joy for our family. The goal of our lifestyle is to imitate our Dad—God, our Heavenly Father. God is faithful in loving us even when we make mistakes, sin against Him, hurt Him deeply, and are slow to learn, and so we must also learn to love and forgive our spouses and children when we believe that they deserve it the least.

Every time we think we have no more strength left to forgive or serve our families again, we meditate on the forgiveness and sacrificial love that Jesus has given us and how He received and accepted us while we were still rejecting Him. When we feel unseen or unappreciated for all we do, we commit our work to the Lord and pray, "Jesus, I'm doing this for *You*," knowing that He always accepts the service done from a loving heart as having been done unto Him (Matthew 25:40). When we are tired and run down, we find our rest in Jesus' light burden (Matthew 11:28–30) and put down all the unnecessary stress and problems He never asked us to carry. And, like Jesus, we fix our eyes on the "joy set before [us]" (Hebrews 12:2), trading our desire for instant gratification in for a long-term view of the joy of watching our children grow into healthy men and women. Serving as a blessing to our families multiplies our joy!

# CHAPTER 7

## *JOY IN THE MIDST OF LONELINESS*

Too often we forfeit our joy in the midst of loneliness. Right now, we're in the middle of a nationwide quarantine due to the Covid-19 virus. Families have to distance themselves from loved ones. Friends are left isolated from other friends. Just about everyone feels very lonely right now, which can even result in suicide for some.

Recently my wife, our daughter, our son-in-law, and our two grandkids went to Virginia for eight days to visit an elderly aunt. I was left here all alone. We live about an hour away from our church, other family members, and our friends. I am a big people person, so needless to say, I was lonely. It would have been easy for me to forfeit my joy, but I chose joy!

I'll admit, I did call Velma often during that week. One day, our three-year-old granddaughter, Iris, was playing games on Nana's phone when I tried to call. Iris decided several times that Papa didn't need to talk anymore! She hung up on me and told Nana,

"Papa doesn't need to talk to you right now!" ☺ I'm pretty sure I would be one miserable hermit then if I weren't deliberate about choosing joy despite having no one to talk to!

One of the greatest trials we encountered as missionaries in the jungle of South America was having our kids go to a boarding school with other missionary kids at a remote mission school base. The many tears we shed as the kids flew away in the small Missionary Aviation Fellowship (MAF) plane on their way to school are vividly engrained in my mind. The moment they took off, we felt very alone, even though we usually had co-workers living nearby. We had to intentionally choose to be joyful, remaining confident in our belief that God was taking care of them afar. It was by far the most difficult part of our ministry. In fact, if we could do it over again, I'm sure we would do things differently. That was truly the only aspect of our work that we considered a sacrifice.

Where we lived in both Venezuela and Brazil, we were located about 300 miles from the nearest frontier town. The only way into where we lived was by small airplane. Knowing how much of a people person I am, our oldest daughter, Candy, said to me one day, "Dad, I don't see how you do this!" My response to Candy was, "I know what you mean, and it's only by God's grace in my life and knowing that these people need an opportunity to hear the gospel. That makes it all worth it because it's not about you or about me; it's about Him." We can and must choose joy, even in loneliness.

I was complaining one day about how much I missed our kids and grandchildren, who were living so far away from us, and Candy said, "Actually, Dad, it's your fault. You raised us this way!" True story. See, some of our kids followed our ministry footprints in different locations: Candy, Brady, and their family are missionaries in South Africa, and Mike, Michelle, and their family are missionaries in Mexico. I miss my spread-out family, but I had to choose joy and praise God that they are living for Him.

One awesome truth is that as Christians, we are NEVER alone!! God is always with us. Intellectually, most of us know that that's true, but deep down we don't really believe that or live as if it is true. We need to regularly remind ourselves of His presence and lean into Him in constant prayer throughout the day until we begin to truly feel Him right here with us. The song "Living Hope" by Phil Wickam is always an encouragement whenever I feel lonely:

> How great the chasm that lay between us
> How high the mountain I could not climb
> In desperation, I turned to heaven
> And spoke Your name into the night
> Then through the darkness, Your
>     loving-kindness
> Tore through the shadows of my soul
> The work is finished, the end is written
> Jesus Christ, my living hope
>
> Who could imagine so great a mercy?
> What heart could fathom such boundless grace?
> The God of ages stepped down from glory
> To wear my sin and bear my shame
> The cross has spoken, I am forgiven
> The King of kings calls me His own
> Beautiful Savior, I'm Yours forever

Jesus Christ, my living hope

Hallelujah, praise the One who set me free
Hallelujah, death has lost its grip on me
You have broken every chain
There's salvation in Your name
Jesus Christ, my living hope

Then came the morning that sealed the promise
Your buried body began to breathe
Out of the silence, the Roaring Lion
Declared the grave has no claim on me
Jesus, Yours is the victory

You may be feeling lonely today, but I can tell
you from experience, don't forfeit your joy. The
following are some encouraging promises by God:

Fear not, for **I am with you**;
be not dismayed, for I am your God;
I will strengthen you, I will help you,
I will uphold you with my righteous right
hand. (Isaiah 41:10)

Be strong and courageous. Do not fear or be in dread of them, for it is the LORD your God who **goes with you. He will not leave you or forsake you.** (Deuteronomy 31:6)

Even though I walk through the valley of the
    shadow of death,
    I will fear no evil,
for **you are with me;**
    your rod and your staff,
    they comfort me. (Psalm 23:4)

## THE STRUGGLE

Of course, loneliness presents an even greater temptation to give in to pride, self-centeredness, and self-focus—it's easy to fixate on ourselves when we feel alone! We have the propensity to feel sorry for ourselves because we are alone. We may begin to believe that no one else has ever had to deal with anything as bad as we do or to shut down our compassion for others and desire to go on loving and serving them when we feel lonely. We do not know how to experience satisfying intimacy with God Himself when we feel cut off from other people.

## THE CHANGE

We need to remember that God is in control. There is no difficulty that can happen to us outside of what He allows, and He will always use it for our good (Romans 8:28). Seasons of loneliness will not last forever, though they can feel like it at the time. Psalm 68:6 says that "God sets the lonely in families" (New International Version), as is consistent with His character; though He lets us suffer through hardship for a time, these trials always result in God liberating, delivering, and restoring us.

Loneliness is still a heavy load to carry, and the Bible does not minimize its sting. Many biblical heroes suffered from loneliness at times, and each of them cried out bitterly against it. Moses was often rejected by the nation of Israel and even once by his own siblings (Numbers 12). Job sat alone in his sorrow after his children died, his wife told him to curse God, and his friends accused him of wrongs he hadn't done. Jeremiah was constantly misunderstood, accused, and punished in ways like being put in the stocks and lowered into a pit by himself.

David had to live on the run for years, cut off from his family and his best friend, Jonathan, and he wrote from inside of a cave:

> Look to the right and see:
>     there is none who takes notice of me;
> no refuge remains to me;
>     no one cares for my soul.
> [5] I cry to you, O Lord;
>     I say, "You are my refuge,
>     my portion in the land of the living." (Psalm 142:4–5)

He still believed that God would restore him, though, as he finished the psalm with a confident assertion: "Bring me out of prison, that I may give thanks to your name! The righteous will surround me, for you will deal bountifully with me" (Psalm 142:7).

When Elijah felt alone, he was caught in so much despair that he didn't even want to go on living! He complained to God:

> It is enough; now, O Lord, take away my life, for I am no better than my fathers... I have been very jealous for the Lord, the God of hosts. For the people of Israel have forsaken your covenant, thrown down your altars, and killed your prophets with the sword, and I, even I only, am left, and they seek my life, to take it away. (1 Kings 19:4,10).

God didn't respond with anger but took care of Elijah's needs by providing food, water, and a new companion in the person of Elisha. God had allowed Elijah to carry out the first part of his ministry alone, but at the right time, He brought along a likeminded friend to join him in doing the work.

Even Jesus suffered from loneliness when none of His friends were able to sit up with Him and grieve in the Garden of Gethsemane. One of His disciples, whose feet He had just finished washing, then came to betray Him, and the rest of the disciples immediately abandoned and denied Him. Sometimes we gloss over that series of abandonment by Jesus' friends because He already knew it would happen, but I don't think that made it hurt any less—Jesus knows all about the deep soul grief of being betrayed by a friend, someone He had been loving and investing in faithfully for three years. On the cross, Jesus was completely rejected, humiliated, and scorned, and He felt even the absence of God Himself! Thankfully, this is a level of loneliness that we as believers will never have to experience.

But Jesus did not let others' opinions or actions affect what He knew to be true, as He trusted God's opinion of Him to outlast the approval of others, as John tells us in John 2:24–25: "But Jesus on his part did not entrust himself to them, because he knew all people [25] and needed no one to bear witness about man, for he himself knew what was in man." He modeled how we can find companionship with God Himself when others abandon us, as David also wrote in Psalm 27:10: "For my father and my mother have forsaken me, but the Lord will take me in." Knowing that we are never alone and learning to find intimacy with God in the stillness helps us press in to experiencing true joy.

## THE NEW FOCUS

We now choose joy, focusing on the fact that we are NEVER alone as a Christian. God promises us He will never leave us or forsake us (Deut. 31:6). Though we may not always feel God with us, during seasons of loneliness we press in even closer to know Him personally and cultivate a deeper intimacy with the only One who can meet us and know us in every single corner of our hearts. Even when we are in good relationships, other people cannot meet our every need or fully satisfy our longing for connection, and loneliness is an opportunity for us to learn to find our ultimate longings satisfied in Jesus alone. Seasons of greater connection with people will come back. But if we use our time in the desert to develop greater closeness with Christ, then we will know how to interact with others in a better way. Instead of using them to fill needs they were never meant to fill, we learn to rejoice in interdependent relationships that ultimately stand on the stability and satisfaction we have in Christ.

# CHAPTER 8

## *JOY IN THE MIDST OF ABUSE*

I wish we never had to so much as talk about abuse, but unfortunately, we live in a broken world. Still, we can choose joy even in the midst of abuse. I'm not in any way suggesting that we should accept, excuse, or welcome abuse! We can, however, take the abuser's power away by not forfeiting our joy. As long as we allow our past abuse to continue flattening our spirits and crippling our lives, we are still in chains, and our abuser is able to keep robbing us of our present tense. The way forward is to reclaim our agency and choose the power of living in joy!

God will hold the abuser accountable, and he or she will not get away with it. I understand this on a personal level, as I was sexually abused as a pre-teenager. The perpetrator was much older than I and has never asked for forgiveness, nor do I expect that to ever happen. I chose to forgive and not to forfeit my joy. It definitely changed my life to view God as a good, good Father, even in horrible circumstances. I was able to see in God's Word that we live in a broken world, and that someday He would make all things right. I trusted that He understood my situation. I learned that when I faced difficult situations, that it helped to look back to the cross, and all that Jesus suffered, willingly, on my behalf.

Corrie ten Boom has said, "Forgiveness is an act of the will, and the will can function regardless of the temperature of the heart." Forgiveness often feels impossible because we have come to believe that it is primarily a matter of emotion, that it means feeling warm fuzzies when we think about the person who abused us and wanting to go out for donuts together. That's not forgiveness; that just sounds like a foolish choice! The good news is, we can forgive the ones who have hurt us even when we don't *feel* very nicely about them, because forgiving means not holding their sins against them and fighting for what is in their best interest. We can turn to God in prayer and talk with Him honestly about our feelings for that person, but then go on to fight on their behalf in intercession, asking Him for the greatest gift they could ever receive—a repentant heart and the mercy and forgiveness of God! The more we pray for those who have persecuted us, the more we desire for them to one day experience God's restoration instead of facing His wrath.

Sexual, physical, and verbal abuse are far more common than we like to admit. Unfortunately, most people suffering from abuse never tell anyone about it. It's important that we are alert to the signs of abuse, pedophiles, predators, etc. Women take responsibility for being abused 100% of the time, even though it is NEVER true! This can make them less likely to open up about what they're going through or reach out for help, because they feel shame for having done something wrong even when they didn't. They need someone to reach out to them and walk along with them through the process of leaving and recovering from an abusive situation. There is hope for healing!

I have counseled many cases of sexual abuse in the past several years. It's utterly tragic that it ever happens in the first place. One young lady who is very special to us suffered brutal sexual abuse by her biological father from the ages of seven to eighteen. It only stopped because she left home for college. She went through a long journey to become capable of choosing joy. She is a very intelligent and pretty national athlete. She still has to face struggles, but she is not forfeiting her joy. She is able to use her story to help other young ladies who have endured the same horror. She has accomplished some amazing things, and we are very proud of her.

Another young lady I know was raped a few different times, and she, too, initially felt worthless and hopeless. Often, survivors of sexual assault think the only way to cope with the mental and emotional pain is to inflict physical pain on themselves through forms of self-harm such as cutting or eating disorders. This young lady is also quite amazing, and over the process of her journey, she has chosen to be joyful. It helped her recognize that God is a Perfect Father, not a reflection of an earthly father. She was able to understand true forgiveness, and that, although, it didn't absolve the perpetrator from their sin, it freed her. She is a pretty and intelligent young lady, and she works hard to walk with Jesus, using her story to help others find healing and choose joy.

I have also counseled women who are being or have been physically or verbally abused by their husbands. There is always hope for reconciliation if an abuser is willing to accept counsel and work through his or her issues, but until that person has an actual change of heart, there should be a separation. You can choose joy in this situation, but no one should stay in an abusive situation. Abusers are just like people addicted to a substance like alcohol or drugs, and addicts all lie! Their only hope of changing is for God to change their hearts. Don't forfeit your joy, and don't stay in an abusive environment. God does and can heal and forgive, but don't think YOU can change them! That's the exact kind of lie that often keeps people trapped in abusive relationships and keeps the abusers from having to face the destructiveness of their own behavior and change.

The song "Voice of Truth" by Casting Crowns can help us choose joy:

Oh what I would do to have
The kind of faith it takes

To climb out of this boat I'm in
Onto the crashing waves

To step out of my comfort zone
To the realm of the unknown where Jesus is
And He's holding out his hand

But the waves are calling out my name
And they laugh at me
Reminding me of all the times
I've tried before and failed
The waves they keep on telling me
Time and time again, "Boy, you'll never win!"
"You'll never win!"

But the voice of truth tells me a different story
And the voice of truth says, "Do not be afraid!"
The voice of truth says, "This is for My glory."
Out of all the voices calling out to me
I will choose to listen and believe
The voice of truth

Oh what I would do to have

The kind of strength it takes

To stand before a giant

With just a sling and a stone

Surrounded by the sound of a thousand

Warriors shaking in their armor

Wishing they'd have had the strength to stand

But the giant's calling out my name

And he laughs at me

Reminding me of all the times

I've tried before and failed

The giant keeps on telling me

Time and time again, "Boy, you'll never win!"

"You'll never win!"

But the voice of truth tells me a different story

And the voice of truth says, "Do not be afraid!"

The voice of truth says, "This is for My glory."

Out of all the voices calling out to me

I will choose to listen and believe

The voice of truth

But the stone was just the right size

To put the giant on the ground

And the waves they don't seem so high

From on top of them looking down

I will soar with the wings of eagles

When I stop and listen to the sound of Jesus

Singing over me


But the voice of truth tells me a different story

And the voice of truth says, "Do not be afraid!"

The voice of truth says, "This is for My glory"

Out of all the voices calling out to me

I will choose to listen and believe

The voice of truth


Because Jesus, You are the voice of truth

And I will listen to You


## THE STRUGGLE


The struggle here is to believe there is hope and that we can still experience joy again. We may listen to the lies that abuse has ingrained into our minds:

that we are worthless, or that we are powerless and forever stuck in this pain. It is hard to envision healing or restoration after abuse.

## THE CHANGE

As in any other situation, our mentality has to change to one of surrendering our hearts, our minds, and our will to the Lord. This may feel like a tall order, especially for someone who is learning to take back the surrender that he or she may have wrongly given to an abuser. We may be tempted to think, "Hey, I'm the victim here! The person who hurt me should have to surrender to God, but *God* owes *me* something after all I've been through." What we misunderstand when we think this way is that surrendering to God does not result in additional burdens or pain but in freedom and joy. 1 Pet. 5:7 admonishes us, "[Cast] all your anxieties on him, for he cares for you." When we give everything we have and everything we are to God, we find ourselves walking lighter without the weight of our previous anxieties, and we discover on the other side of that surrender a good Father who deeply cares for us—and shows it through His actions!

Since abuse often damages our view of both God and ourselves, joy comes when we shift our understanding of who God is and who we are. We must recognize that God is not like our abuser(s). They manipulated and controlled us; God gives us freedom (Galatians 5:1) and is faithful to keep His word to us, exactly as He said it (Isaiah 55:10–11). They deceived and lied to us; God always tells us the truth (Proverbs 30:5). They imitated Satan in his work of stealing, killing, and destroying (John 10:10), but God is the great Redeemer whose work is to "bind up the brokenhearted, to proclaim liberty to the captives" (Isaiah 61:1), and to raise the dead with new life (Matthew 11:5).

One passage that helps tremendously in separating out the difference between our abusers and God is Ezekiel 34. Although this passage is specifically speaking to religious leaders who abused the people they were supposed to be shepherding, it is still helpful with regard to any kind of abuse. It is helpful to read the whole chapter, as God outlines here both how He *feels* about seeing His people be abused and what He intends to *do* about it:

> Son of man, prophesy against the shepherds of Israel; prophesy, and say to them, even to the shepherds, Thus says the Lord God: Ah, shepherds of Israel who have been feeding yourselves! Should not shepherds feed the sheep? [3] You eat the fat, you clothe yourselves with the wool, you slaughter the fat ones, but you do not feed the sheep. [4] The weak you have not strengthened, the sick you have not healed, the injured you have not bound up, the strayed you have not brought back, the lost you have not sought, and with force and harshness you have ruled them. [5] So they were scattered, because there was no shepherd, and they became food for all the wild beasts. My sheep were scattered; [6] they wandered over all the mountains and on every high hill. My sheep were scattered over all the face of the earth, with none to search or seek for them.

[7] "Therefore, you shepherds, hear the word of the Lord: [8] As I live, declares the Lord God, surely because my sheep have become a prey, and my sheep have become food for all the wild beasts, since there was no shepherd, and because my shepherds have not searched for my sheep, but the shepherds have fed themselves, and have not fed my sheep, [9] therefore, you shepherds, hear the word of the Lord: [10] Thus says the Lord God, Behold, I am against the shepherds, and I will require my sheep at their hand and put a stop to their feeding the sheep. No longer shall the shepherds feed themselves. I will rescue my sheep from their mouths, that they may not be food for them.

[11] "For thus says the Lord God: Behold, I, I myself will search for my sheep and will seek them out. [12] As a shepherd seeks out his flock when he is among his sheep that have been scattered, so will I seek out my sheep, and I will rescue them from all places where they have been scattered on a day of clouds and thick

darkness. [13] And I will bring them out from the peoples and gather them from the countries, and will bring them into their own land. And I will feed them on the mountains of Israel, by the ravines, and in all the inhabited places of the country. [14] I will feed them with good pasture, and on the mountain heights of Israel shall be their grazing land. There they shall lie down in good grazing land, and on rich pasture they shall feed on the mountains of Israel. [15] I myself will be the shepherd of my sheep, and I myself will make them lie down, declares the Lord God. [16] I will seek the lost, and I will bring back the strayed, and I will bind up the injured, and I will strengthen the weak, and the fat and the strong I will destroy.[a] I will feed them in justice.

[17] "As for you, my flock, thus says the Lord God: Behold, I judge between sheep and sheep, between rams and male goats. [18] Is it not enough for you to feed on the good pasture, that you must tread down with your feet the rest of

your pasture; and to drink of clear water, that you must muddy the rest of the water with your feet? ¹⁹ And must my sheep eat what you have trodden with your feet, and drink what you have muddied with your feet?

²⁰ "Therefore, thus says the Lord God to them: Behold, I, I myself will judge between the fat sheep and the lean sheep. ²¹ Because you push with side and shoulder, and thrust at all the weak with your horns, till you have scattered them abroad, ²² I will rescue[b] my flock; they shall no longer be a prey. And I will judge between sheep and sheep. ²³ And I will set up over them one shepherd, my servant David, and he shall feed them: he shall feed them and be their shepherd. ²⁴ And I, the Lord, will be their God, and my servant David shall be prince among them. I am the Lord; I have spoken.

²⁵ "I will make with them a covenant of peace and banish wild beasts from the land, so that they may dwell securely in the wilderness and

sleep in the woods. ²⁶ And I will make them and the places all around my hill a blessing, and I will send down the showers in their season; they shall be showers of blessing. ²⁷ And the trees of the field shall yield their fruit, and the earth shall yield its increase, and they shall be secure in their land. And they shall know that I am the Lord, when I break the bars of their yoke, and deliver them from the hand of those who enslaved them. ²⁸ They shall no more be a prey to the nations, nor shall the beasts of the land devour them. They shall dwell securely, and none shall make them afraid. ²⁹ And I will provide for them renowned plantations so that they shall no more be consumed with hunger in the land, and no longer suffer the reproach of the nations. ³⁰ And they shall know that I am the Lord their God with them, and that they, the house of Israel, are my people, declares the Lord God. ³¹ And you are my sheep, human sheep of my pasture, and I am your God, declares the Lord God."

God is beyond angry when He sees His people abused—He is livid! He will not stand silently by to watch them be trampled upon. Though this can be hard to see when He has already allowed the abuse to occur, we need to come to understand that He is waiting to execute His wrath on abusers so that the maximum number of people can turn to Jesus for mercy instead (Matthew 13:24–30; 2 Peter 3:9). He has not forgotten you, and He will act with both justice and mercy—either through the justice poured out on His Son on the cross, or in justice for an unrepentant abuser who never turns to Christ for mercy.

But Ezekiel 34 doesn't stop there; it also shows that Jesus, the Good Shepherd, has promised to restore us and care for us tenderly, meeting our needs and blessing us abundantly. This is the Father's heart for us: to "lay down His life for the sheep" (John 10:11). The more we encounter the anger, the justice, and the tenderness of God, the more we are able to step into joy.

Abuse also lies to us about our own identities; it says that we are powerless, worthless, shameful, and used up. We need to spend time absorbing what God's

Word says about us to help us believe that because of Jesus, we *do* have the power to choose a new way of thinking and to embrace the fullness of restoration in Christ! There are too many verses about our identity in Christ to mention all of them, but here is a brief list to get you started:

| | |
|---|---|
| John 1:12 | I am God's child (1 John 3:1–3) |
| 1 Cor. 3:16 | I am God's temple |
| 2 Cor. 6:1 | I am God's coworker (1 Cor. 3:9) |
| Eph. 1:1 | I am a saint |
| Eph. 2:6 | I have been raised up and I am seated with Christ |
| Eph. 2:10 | I am God's workmanship |
| Phil. 3:20 | I am a citizen of heaven (Eph. 2:6) |
| John 15:15 | I am Christ's friend |
| Rom. 5:1 | I have been justified |
| 1 Cor. 6:20 | I have been bought with a price; I belong to God |
| Eph. 2:19 | I am a member of God's household and a fellow citizen with the rest of the saints |

| | |
|---|---|
| Col. 1:14 | I have been redeemed and forgiven of all my sins |
| Col. 2:10 | I am complete in Christ |
| Rom. 8:35–40 | I cannot be separated from the love of God |
| Rom. 8:1 | I am free forever from condemnation |
| Col. 1:13 | I have been delivered from the domain of darkness and transferred to the kingdom of Christ |
| Phil. 1:6 | I am confident that the good work God has begun in me will be perfected |
| Phil. 4:13 | I can do all things through Him who strengthens me |
| 2 Tim. 1:7 | I have not been given the spirit of fear, but of power, love and a sound mind |
| Heb. 4:16 | I can find grace and mercy in time of need |
| 1 Jn. 5:18 | I am born of God and the evil one cannot touch me |

As we rediscover the truth of Scripture about who we are, we can imitate Jesus' example by trusting that what He says about us is our true identity, not what other people say (John 2:24–25) or what our own hearts and self-critical spirits say in accusation (1 John 3:20). This empowers us to stand up and make the choice to step back into God's gift of joy!

## THE NEW FOCUS

We now choose joy because we know that we are not alone in this. Jesus understands everything we could ever go through, including the horrors of abuse. Remember, He Himself was abused: whipped, beaten, spit upon, mocked, insulted, rejected, tortured, neglected, undressed, and even killed. As Hebrews 4:15 says, "For we do not have a high priest who is unable to sympathize with our weaknesses, but one who in every respect has been tempted as we are, yet without sin." Yet He overcame, forgave His abusers, and did not return as a permanent victim but as a reigning, glorious, and life-filled conqueror!

Jesus now offers that victory and resurrection life to us as well, and no horror or degradation we have experienced is too great for Him to cleanse, purify, and restore. 2 Corinthians 7:6a reminds us that "God comforts the downcast." In Christ, we receive not only comfort but also new life and a fresh start! We are remade and defined not by the way that others have treated us but by how Jesus Himself interacts with us: He chooses us, He cares for us, He protects us, He provides for us, He honors us, He cherishes us, He lifts our heads, and He fills us with goodness and strength. That's why we can choose joy. He is our source of JOY!

# CHAPTER 9

## *JOY IN THE MIDST OF SICKNESS*

We live in a broken world, and we all suffer from sickness at times, sometimes more severe than others. For most of us, sickness will eventually take our lives. Even so, let's not forfeit our joy!

We have a good friend in our church, an elderly man who suffered from cancer. But what an amazing testimony he had in the midst of that suffering. He was an incredible example of choosing to be joyful. He was intentional about it. Jerry always had a solid perspective on life, and it was no surprise when he found out that he had terminal cancer, that he didn't forfeit his joy. He made the intentional choice to "end" life on this earth well, reflecting the goodness of His Savior. He planned out his own memorial and it all centered on the goodness of his relationship with Jesus Christ. He mentioned that he never wanted to become a "grouchy old man." He wanted young and old alike, to see Jesus in his lifestyle.

I've had malaria several times. One time when I was in Brazil, living far from any town, I ended up with three kinds of malaria at the same time (P. vivax, P. ovale, and P. falciprium). I took several different treatments but just couldn't get rid of it. I have a difficult time sitting still. In fact, when I was a young man, my mom used to tell me that God was going to teach me to slow down one day. ☺ One of our coworkers in the village was building their house at that time, and of course I wanted to help. I would go over early in the morning and work until noon, and, without fail, by then I could no longer stand. I would have high fevers and shake intolerably, so I would have to lie down. This went on for an entire year. It was clear to me that I could forfeit my joy and complain about it, which wasn't going to help anyway, or I could choose joy. I chose joy. After a year, someone gave me some medicine called Palugil, and lo and behold, it got rid of my malaria!

Once when I was coaching basketball, my wife and I traveled for an away game. Our two youngest kids (at the time, anyway) stayed behind with some of our friends. Jim was in first grade, and I made it clear to him that he was not to ride his bicycle in the street. (He called it the airstrip—it's what he could relate to as a missionary kid from the jungle. ☺) The game was five hours away. We had finally arrived, checked the players into the hotel, and left for the gym.

Just as we pulled up to the entrance, someone came up to me and said, "Are you Coach Griffis?" I replied, "Yes, I am." He said, "You need to call the hospital in Panama City right away. I can't tell you what it's about." I finally got him to tell me that Jim had been hit by a van and was in the hospital and that they wouldn't do anything for him until I got there. So Velma and I caught a ride all the way back to Panama City and went directly to the hospital. Of course we were concerned, but as we prayed, we told God we trusted Him, and we didn't forfeit our joy. The doctors commented on how calm we were, which gave us the opportunity to share our testimony with them.

By God's providence, Jim's schoolteacher was on duty at the hospital, and she took responsibility for him. He was fine, some bruising but no broken bones. He later told us he wasn't "riding in the street." He was just "turning around in the street." Jim's perception of what it meant to follow the rules was amusing, but the nearly-fatal seriousness of the situation wasn't. A van hit him and sent him ten feet into the air, completely knocking out the grill of the van and crunching the bike up underneath it. The mercy of God was written into Jim's every unbroken bone!

We were spared much grief that day, but unfortunately, God doesn't always deliver us from having to suffer through the agony of injury, sickness, and disease. It often feels like for every miracle that comes, another ten tragedies take place. There's no getting away from the universal human experience of sickness.

Sometimes a series of events can cause mental illness. This can become exhausting for the caregiver. Even then, we must keep things in perspective and remember that those suffering from mental illness are usually not being difficult on purpose. We must choose joy. Generally, once the individual is on the right medication, he or she can function very well. He or she can also choose to be joyful.

The song "More Than Anything" by Natalie
Grant gives words to the prayer many of us are
grasping for in times of deep agony:

I know if you wanted to
You could wave your hand
Spare me this heartache and change your plan
And I know any second
You could take my pain away
But even if you don't I pray

Help me want the Healer more than the healing
Help me want the Savior more than the saving
Help me want the Giver more than the giving
Help me want you Jesus more than anything

You know more than anyone
That my flesh is weak
And you know I'd give anything for a remedy
And I'll ask a thousand more times
To set me free today
Oh but even if you don't I pray

Help me want the Healer more than the healing
Help me want the Savior more than the saving
Help me want the Giver more than the giving
Oh Help me want you Jesus
More than anything

When I'm desperate and my hearts overcome
All that I need you've already done
When I'm desperate and my hearts overcome
All that I need you've already done

Oh Jesus Help me want you
More than anything

Help me want the Healer more than the healing
Help me want the Savior more than the saving
Help me want the Giver more than the giving
Help me want you Jesus more than anything
Help me want you Jesus more than anything

Sometimes God doesn't choose to heal us from sickness, but we can choose to be joyful in the sickness, bringing honor and glory to Him.

## THE STRUGGLE

A common struggle with sickness is that we are focused primarily (or even exclusively!) on the healing itself rather than continuing to seek God for His own sake and consider Christ Himself our reward, regardless of whether He heals us or not. Therefore, we may not allow our joy in the midst of pain to speak of God's goodness and encourage others.

We also want to be in control of everything, and sickness is an unwelcome reminder that we are definitely not in control. Not only does it cause pain and inconvenience, but it also provokes fear and loss of a feeling of security.

## THE CHANGE

We acknowledge that we are not in control, and we surrender our hearts and minds to Jesus. The Apostle Paul speaks about learning to accept his own weakness in 2 Corinthians 12:7–10:

So to keep me from becoming conceited because of the surpassing greatness of the revelations, a thorn was given me in the flesh, a messenger of Satan to harass me, to keep me from becoming conceited. [8] Three times I pleaded with the Lord about this, that it should leave me. [9] But he said to me, "My grace is sufficient for you, for my power is made perfect in weakness." Therefore I will boast all the more gladly of my weaknesses, so that the power of Christ may rest upon me. [10] For the sake of Christ, then, I am content with weaknesses, insults, hardships, persecutions, and calamities. For when I am weak, then I am strong.

We don't know if Paul's thorn in the flesh was a physical illness or some other kind of life problem, but this passage certainly rings true for us when we walk through the agony of sickness. When we are healthy and not experiencing any major setbacks, it is easy for us to become proud and to believe that we are in charge of our own lives, that we can do anything, like the builders of the Tower of Babel believed. In illness, however, God gives us the opportunity to humble ourselves and acknowledge Him as the source of all that we have. Furthermore, He supplies us with constant grace and the internal power of Christ so that we are never lacking any good spiritual gift. Being stripped of all the worldly crutches we so often rely on brings us into closer contact with the grace and power of God, where we are raised up into maturity in Christ and revitalized within.

Another truth we can meditate on in the midst of sickness is that we are never alone in our pain: Christ has suffered through much greater physical pain and death, so He understands our sorrow when we bear such a load. Isaiah refers to Jesus as the man of sorrows "acquainted with grief" who "was pierced for our transgressions" and "crushed for our iniquities" (Isaiah 53:3,5). Therefore, He is able to sympathize with us in our own suffering (Hebrews 4:15), and it matters to Him when we are in pain.

Finally, we cling to the promise that sickness will never have the final word over our lives, even if it ends in death. Like the earth itself, we groan not only in pain but also with our longing for the new creation

(Romans 8:22), where God has promised that we will live in glorious resurrected bodies (1 Corinthians 15:35–55) with no more pain, tears, or suffering (Revelation 21:4). Sickness helps us shift our focus from achieving everything we want in this life to setting our hope on the resurrection life to come (2 Corinthians 4:16), and we can choose joy knowing that God's promises for us are of life, health, and complete restoration.

## THE NEW FOCUS

We now choose joy in the midst of sickness, encouraging others as they see us rejoicing in the Lord always. Though sickness feels limiting and debilitating, we recognize that it simply changes our opportunities, because God can actually give us a bigger and more powerful platform to show others God's peace and grace in our lives as we continue testifying to His goodness. We cast ourselves fully upon the power and protection of God, choosing to believe that His grace is sufficient for us. Instead of crumpling into despair, we stand firm in our resolve to know Jesus and find His joy even when we are in pain!

# CHAPTER 10

## *JOY IN THE MIDST OF DIVORCE*

What happens when our marriages begin to suffer and break down, and it feels like there is no hope for going back to the way things used to be? Sometimes it feels like the only way to choose joy in that situation is to choose to leave the marriage itself! That would make us much happier, right? But God's design for marriage has not changed. His blueprint for marriage is "till death do us part." I truly believe that resolution is always possible for a marriage **IF** both husband and wife are willing to humble themselves and work it out, surrendering their will to the Lord.

I worked with an older couple where one partner had had multiple affairs over a long period of time, unknown to the other. I'll call them Frank and Polly. Polly had thought that their marriage was better than ever, not knowing about any of the affairs. The kids were all grown and no longer living at home. When the affairs came to light, they were devastating to the entire family.

I worked with Frank first, the one who had actually sinned against the other. Frank genuinely confessed and repented from his sin. Unfortunately, Frank then thought everything should simply go back to normal. I told him that it didn't work that way. He was not the victim, and he had to allow Polly space and time to forgive and heal. Praise the Lord, in this case they were able to reconcile with time and are still happily married—better than ever before! They are choosing joy. What helped Polly to choose to forgive and find healing, was recognizing how much God had forgiven her of her own sins. She also realized that forgiveness is a choice, and that it gave Frank and opportunity to, once again, build trust, since he had genuinely repented. He began to romance her again, and they consistently looked to God's Word on what a healthy marriage looked like. They are stronger than ever. That being said, there are times when the marriage cannot be resolved due to issues like abuse or other kinds of sin. Scripturally, God makes allowance for divorce in the case of unfaithfulness (Matthew 19:9). But Jesus upgraded the qualifications of what it means to be faithful when He said, "But I say to you that everyone who looks at a woman with lustful intent has already committed adultery with her in his heart" (Matthew 5:28).

Infidelity is a tricky issue, because in these cases, the Bible gives us permission to divorce but does not say we have to do so. Many Christian couples are able to do the grueling work of forgiving and reestablishing a marriage after all kinds of infidelity, from problems with pornography to affairs. But it's no walk in the park to do, because infidelity reveals what is primarily an issue of the *heart*. To rebuild a truly intimate relationship of trust and honesty, the spouse who has been sinned against must choose forgiveness and letting the past go, and the spouse who sinned must deal with the deeper heart issues that led him or her to seek an escape from pain through sexual sin. Unfortunately, no person has the power to change another, and many times, a person caught in habitual lying, infidelity, or abuse is unwilling to acknowledge the real problem or take steps toward repentance and change. Even in a situation where a divorce is unavoidable, we still must choose JOY!

No one should allow him- or herself to be remain in an abusive situation where he or she can be injured or one of the children is abused. God can change a heart, but this needs to be done in separation. As long as the couple caught in a cycle of abuse remains together, it will be hard for them to snap out of familiar patterns, and neither one will be able to do the slow heart work of change as long as they're continuing to experience active abuse. The spouse being abused obviously needs to stay in a safe place until it is clear that the marriage is a healthy environment again, but even the abuser needs space to confront his or her own sin and buried wounds alone before he or she will be able to reconcile in a genuine and lasting way. This kind of change may sound impossible, and unfortunately, in a high number of cases it never happens (because again, we cannot control others' decisions or growth!). But because of Jesus, it *is* possible and does sometimes take place.

Divorce should never be our first option, because God loves marriage!! After all, He instituted it. He said it was "not good for man (Adam) to be alone" (Genesis 2:18, New International Version), so

He created a wife (Eve) out of Adam's rib. He also told them to procreate and thus populate the earth. Marriage is God's sacred plan not only to mature each individual spouse but also to bring about blessing for the earth.

Because we live in a fallen world, divorce does happen, sometimes even to believers. But the Bible only gives grounds for divorce in very few cases, and we know that it is *not* God's desire for any of us. Even when divorce seems preferable or unavoidable, we can learn to choose joy within the context of a struggling marriage and pursue the next stage of joy: the joy of reconciliation!

## THE STRUGGLE

We are prone to be selfish, unbending, stubborn, and self-centered. It takes hard work and humility to make a marriage thrive.

When a marriage does fail, both people enter into a grieving process and undergo significant life change, which causes stress and can make them perceive a loss of control in their lives. They may feel shame or guilt for being divorced, and the social stigma might strain their friendships as well.

## THE CHANGE

We need to ignore pop culture's opinions and standards for what's right and wrong and follow the true standards found in God's Word. For those considering divorce, Jesus' words in 5:32 are clear: any divorce "except on the ground of sexual immorality" sets people up for committing adultery.

God's Word paves a path forward toward restoration of a marriage by shifting our perspective from "What can I get out of my spouse?" to "What can I give my spouse," as Paul advises believers who are married to non-believers to stay in the marriage if possible, because if they stay, they may be able to serve as a testimony to their spouses and lead them to the Lord (1 Corinthians 7:12–16). Even for marriages between believers, a similar attitude can help them stick it out through hardship as each spouse makes his or her motivation for remaining in the marriage to serve as a *blessing* to the other spouse instead of to find personal gratification through someone else. Though that kind of self-sacrificial love is grueling work and involves many moments of pain, it also leads to true, deep joy.

Hosea modeled this kind of Christ-like love by remaining faithful to his wife, Gomer, even when she was repeatedly unfaithful to him. In fact, he knew before he ever married her that she would commit adultery against him, and he still obeyed God and chose to make her the object of his affection and the mother of his children! Then, Hosea sought her out with the man she had chosen over him and was willing to pay for the right to take her home—he considered her worth spending precious money and resources on, after all that she had done to him! God led Hosea to demonstrate such preposterous and seemingly foolish love as an object lesson of how He has loved us and had mercy on us through Christ. Do you think that Hosea or Jesus chose forgiveness and love for those that had rejected them without any emotional pain involved? Of course not—pain was part of the bride price they paid to win back Gomer and the church. But because we have received such extravagant love from

Christ, we can apply it within our own broken marriages and find joy in giving ourselves away, even for a spouse whom we feel does not deserve it.

For some, however, divorce is unavoidable or has already occurred. This does not mean they are excluded from choosing and experiencing Jesus' joy in the aftermath of heartbreak. We know that in Christ, we have a new start, as God's mercies "are new every morning" (Lamentations 3:22–23). We are not alone or discarded, for God Himself stands as the loving husband watching over His people as a bride (Isaiah 54:5, Ephesians 5:25–27). Divorce does not define us or separate us from the mercy and love of God. As a wise woman once said, "I had to learn that God cared about *me* more than He cared about my marriage!" Choosing to forgive the sins that have been committed against us, confess and repent of the sins that we have committed, and recognize the opportunity for new life that God offers us opens the door for us to choose joy in moving forward.

### THE NEW FOCUS

In marriage, we now learn to focus our hopes for satisfaction and fulfillment on Christ and not on our spouse—a role that no human can ever fill! We take responsibility for our own actions and sins, confess regularly and with humility, maintain full honesty and vulnerability with our spouse, and seek ways in which we can be a blessing and serve our spouse's best interests instead of our own. We forgive frequently and work through our own personal issues. Even if our marriage never seems to get easier, we press on, keeping our hope fixed upon the reward we have in Christ instead of the reward of a white picket fence.

For those who have seen a marriage come to an end, we remember that divorce is not the end of the world. Choose joy and move on, serving God with all your heart. You are not cut off from God, and He still has more restoration in store for you!

# CHAPTER 11

## *FINAL THOUGHTS ON NOT FORFEITING OUR JOY*

Why would anyone want to forfeit their joy? **Has forfeiting your joy ever made anything better?!** Of course not! So why not go ahead and choose joy? If my complaining or forfeiting joy isn't going to solve anything, why go there? It doesn't seem rational to me. There are things I can control and do something about, and then there are a multitude of things that are out of my control, so I need to take those to the Lord and leave them there.

Philippians 4:4–9 reminds us of the power that we have in choosing to continue rejoicing in the Lord and focusing our minds on Him:

> Rejoice in the LORD always; again I will say, rejoice. ⁵ Let your reasonableness be known to everyone. The LORD is at hand; ⁶ do not be anxious about anything, but in everything by prayer and supplication with thanksgiving let

your requests be made known to God. [7] And the peace of God, which surpasses all understanding, will guard your hearts and your minds in Christ Jesus.

[8] Finally, brothers, whatever is true, whatever is honorable, whatever is just, whatever is pure, whatever is lovely, whatever is commendable, if there is any excellence, if there is anything worthy of praise, think about these things. [9] What you have learned and received and heard and seen in me—practice these things, and the God of peace will be with you.

**We can change how and what we think—choose JOY!**
The command here in Scripture seems pretty clear cut to me.

God has handed each of us a megaphone, and we are all using our lives to shout out a message to the ever-listening world around us. What are you shouting out through your choices?

In the midst of anxiety and depression, choose joy!

In the midst of losing a loved one, choose joy!

In the midst of change, choose joy!

In the midst of family life, choose joy!

In the midst of loneliness, choose joy!

In the midst of abuse, choose joy!

In the midst of sickness, choose joy!

In the midst of divorce, choose joy!

JOY is one key component of the fruit of the Spirit. If we are in the Spirit, we are exercising joy!

## I CHOOSE

"I Choose" is an excerpt from *The Glory of Christmas* by Charles Swindoll, Max Lucado, and Charles Colson. It reminds us that we are not victims of the circumstances that life throws our way, but that each of us has agency in choosing how we respond:

**I choose love....**

No occasion justifies hatred; no injustice warrants bitterness. I choose love. Today I will love God and what God loves.

**I choose joy...**

I will invite my God to be the God of circumstance. I will refuse the temptation to be cynical... the tool of the lazy thinker. I will refuse to see people as anything less than human beings, created by God. I will refuse to see any problem as anything less than an opportunity to see God.

**I choose peace....**

I will live forgiven. I will forgive so that I may live.

**I choose patience....**

I will overlook the inconveniences of the world. Instead of cursing the one who takes my place, I'll invite him to do so. Rather then complain that the wait is too long, I will thank God for a moment to pray. Instead of clenching my fist at new assignments, I will face them with joy and courage.

**I choose kindness...**

I will be kind to the poor, for they are alone. Kind to the rich, for they are afraid. And kind to the unkind, for such is how God has treated me.

**I choose goodness...**

I will go without a dollar before I take a dishonest one. I will be overlooked before I boast. I will confess before I will accuse. I choose goodness.

**I choose faithfulness...**

Today I will keep my promises. My debtors will not regret their trust. My associates will not question my word. My wife will not question my love. And my children will never fear that their father will not come home.

**I choose gentleness...**

Nothing is won by force. I choose to be gentle. If I raise my voice, may it only be in praise. If I clench my fist, may it only be in prayer. If I make a demand, may it only be of myself.

**I choose self-control...**

I am a spiritual being. After this body is dead, my spirit will soar. I refuse to let what will rot rule the eternal. I choose self-control. I will be drunk only by joy. I will be impassioned only by my faith. I will be influenced only by God. I will be taught only by Christ. I choose self-control.

**Love, joy, peace, patience, kindness, goodness,**

faithfulness, gentleness, and self-control. To
these I commit my day. If I succeed, I will give
thanks. If I fail, I will seek his grace. And then,
when this day is done, I will place my head on
the pillow and rest.

## Anyway

You might be familiar with the following poem,
which is usually called "Anyway" and thought to have
been written by Mother Teresa. Actually, it was
written by a college student named Kent M. Keith in
1968 under the original title "The Paradoxical
Commandments." It gives another good snapshot into
how we can use our free will to respond well to all
kinds of negative situations:

> People are often unreasonable, illogical, and
> self-centered. Forgive them anyway.

> If you are kind, people may accuse you of selfish
> ulterior motives. Be kind anyway.

If you are successful, you will win false friends and true enemies. Succeed anyway.

If you are honest and frank, people may cheat you. Be honest and frank anyway.

What you spend years building, someone could destroy overnight. Build anyway.

If you find serenity and happiness, they may be jealous. Be happy anyway.

The good you do today, people will often forget tomorrow. Do good anyway.

Give the world the best you have, and it may never be enough. Give the world the best you've got anyway.

You see, in the final analysis, it is between you and your God. It was never between you and them anyway.

# NEW FOCUS

The only way through is to surrender our hearts to the Lord, being obedient to His commands. This often strikes our stubborn hearts as the *last* thing we would ever want to do in order to find joy, but the more we realize that God is a good, good Father, the more we trust that His intentions toward us are good. As we give ourselves and our wills to God, we find release from the prison and torture of our own pride, rebellion, and tendency toward choosing brokenness. Knowing Jesus is what leads us to joy. Obeying God is what leads us to life and wellness.

We need to refocus the megaphones of our lives and use them to joyfully point to Jesus. Our attitude is contagious, and the more we train our hearts on Christ in all moments, the louder we proclaim the good news of Jesus to everyone we know. Joy is a choice, so don't forfeit your joy!